Jesus, the Master Psychologist

Dr. Ray Guarendi

Jesus, The Master Psychologist

Listen to Him

EWTN PUBLISHING, INC.
Irondale, Alabama

EWTN Publishing, Inc.
5817 Old Leeds Road, Irondale, AL 35210

Distributed by Sophia Institute Press, Box 5284, Manchester, NH 03108.

paperback ISBN 978-1-68278-236-1

ebook ISBN 978-1-68278-237-8

Library of Congress Control Number: 2021936815

First printing

If Christianity should happen to be true, then it is quite impossible that those who know the truth and those who don't should be equally well equipped for leading a good life. Knowledge of the facts must make a difference to one's actions.

—C. S. Lewis, "Man or Rabbit?"

Contents

1. Who Is This Man? 3

2. An IQ Too High 9

3. Unworthy of Self-Worth? 13

4. Humility Is Reality 17

5. Childlike, Not Childish 23

6. Seek to Be Meek 29

7. *Cui Bono?* 33

8. True Gold 39

9. Mouth Control 43

10. Mind Control 49

11. Welcome a Child, Welcome Jesus 53

12. A Chip off the Old Block 61

13. Inflated Value 67

14. Stop It 77

15. Am I Good or What? 83

16. The "J" Word 91

17. Give and You'll Get 99

18. A Hard Teaching. 103

19. Small Words; Big Effect 111

20. A Cheeky Response 117

21. Death? When? 123

About the Author 131

Jesus, the Master Psychologist

1

Who Is This Man?

"Jesus was a good man." That is false. "Jesus was a good man." That is true. So, which is it? How can Jesus be a good man yet not a good man? To echo Mr. Spock, the ultra-rational character from the old television series Star Trek,[1] "logic would dictate" that something can't be both A and not A at the same time. Unless that something, or in this case, that someone, is the God-man.

If Jesus were only a man, but one Who claimed to be divine, then His goodness is in doubt, especially since He wasn't content to be just another god among the then-accepted pantheon of gods, but the God—the Creator and Ruler of the Universe. He accepted worship, professed no beginning, and promised to one day judge the whole world. He talked and acted like He was God, not once or twice in a fleeting burst of self-exaltation, but consistently. He allowed no room for anyone to see Him as a sage, guru, heady philosopher, or just a plain nice guy.

Psychologists use a "clinical interview" to assess a person's mental state—the quality and clarity of his thinking. Not uncommonly, an individual may be cautious at first with his answers. He suspects

[1] The original series, created by Gene Roddenberry, aired on NBC, 1966–1969.

they are being analyzed, so he strives to sound "normal." Should he slowly relax, he may become more open. Suppose he confides, "I'm going to tell you something no one else knows: I'm George Washington, I'm back from the dead, and I'm going to run for president."

"I'm George Washington" is, in psychiatry-speak, a delusion. A delusion is a belief that collides head-on with reality, one that is stubbornly unyielding to reason or persuasion. It is a sign of psychosis or a severe mental disorder.

If Jesus were not God but sincerely believed He was, then He was seriously disturbed. Not that this would infect His every thought; delusional thinking doesn't necessarily warp all reality. It would, however, prove that at the inner core of His being—His self-identity—Jesus was gravely mistaken or misguided. Furthermore, if He knew He wasn't God but claimed so to gather credulous followers, then He was an imposter, leaving grave doubt about His goodness.

If Jesus were merely human, then His teachings can be accepted or rejected. He is another name on a long list of life-guides—Buddha, Gandhi, Tony Robbins, Mr. Rogers. No matter how profound He may have sounded at times, Jesus was still someone Who was delusional or deceptive.

But there is another possibility: Jesus is Who He said He is. He is God among us. Reason and evidence make a strong case for this, one that is persuasive if examined free of pre-conceived biases. Honest searching has brought countless former skeptics to the Faith. Such searching is beyond the scope of this book, but here are a few pieces of reasoning which point in that direction.

Science can prove nor disprove Jesus' divinity. Science observes, sets up hypotheses, and tests them. Jesus' presence on earth is a historical event. It lies beyond the scientific method. It can't be replicated.

Christianity exists. How did it begin, and what—or who—sustains it? Legions of rulers, dictators, and powerful societies have determined to crush it. Yet it endures. The Catholic Church is the oldest institution in the Western World, having outlived all of its former persecutors. How? If the Gospel authors were concocting clever and highly-embellished stories to dupe a gullible audience, they weren't very good at it. In fact, they were downright pathetic. They showed little knowledge of Propaganda 101, which instructs never, ever to depict your founders and luminaries in a bad light.

On the contrary, the Gospels are riddled with incidents of the apostles sounding and acting dense, confused, self-seeking, and frightened. Their supreme leader, in all four Gospels, denies several times that he even knows Jesus, despite having been awed by His miracles and previously proclaiming Him the Son of God. Why would anyone write such defamatory depictions of the movement's headmen? Just leave those images out. Unless, of course, they really happened and writing the truth was all that mattered to these men.

Something earth-shattering must have arisen to transform a bunch of frightened, cowering ex-followers into intrepid challengers of the autocratic Jewish and Roman authorities. And who preached boldly until, as other historical sources report, they died as tortured martyrs, not once forsaking their Master. Who would die for a manipulative liar or a foolish myth? Scripture proclaims that the earth-shattering miracle which radically converted the apostles was Jesus rising from the dead.

The only apostle to die a natural death was John, who in his later years was exiled by an oppressive Roman emperor. Even so, he still refused to renounce Christ, which would have been his "get out of jail free card."

A seemingly minor but significant sign of the Gospels' truth is the account of the women's arrival at the tomb on Sunday morning. Women were not considered credible witnesses in that society. They weren't allowed to testify in court. Why, then, would the Gospels report that women were the first to tell of the missing body? If their aim were to weave a believable tale, then they should have written that fearless men had confronted the tomb's guards and found that Jesus was missing. Again, one narrates that the women were first at the tomb only if it is true, risking heavy cultural skepticism.

A widespread cliché is, "Faith does not depend upon reason or logic. Faith is solely a decision to believe." One well-known Christian counters with, "God has given us enough evidence to have a reasonable faith but not enough to live by reason alone."[2]

Judging Jesus' identity is not akin to a criminal court proceeding, where a just ruling demands evidence beyond doubt. It is more like a civil court, where the preponderance of evidence decides the verdict.

Once one has concluded in heart and mind that Jesus is divine, then other conclusions logically follow:

1. *He is a good man.* God sharing human flesh can only be good. More so, He is a perfect man, unable to misinform or mislead. He possesses complete insight into the human psyche, with all its potential for virtue and vice.

2. *He doesn't have a split personality.* He can't be otherworldly-wise while uttering absurdities. Some of His teachings can't be delusional while others are "the way, the truth, and the life." Scattered among His words would be those tainted by a defective self-identity. They would evoke a skeptical raised eyebrow, a "Huh?"

One needn't be a therapist to recognize someone's drift from reality. Nowhere are Jesus' teachings remotely out-of-kilter. One may choose not to believe them or not to live by them, but they aren't unreasonable.

3. *He deserves obedience.* He can't be ignored or rejected without unexpected or unwanted consequences. When He instructs, "Think this way and not that way," or "Act this way and not that

---

[2] Ravi Zacharias, Twitter.com.

way," He is doing so for our own good. He knows exactly how we would best live, just as He designed us.

What if His wisdom contradicts that of other "wise" teachers? What if it is deemed better for the distant past rather than for the present? What if it challenges prevailing views of enlightenment? What if it condemns the reigning morals of our society? Should the whole world disagree with Jesus, His is the only voice that matters. All other voices, no matter how educated or sophisticated they may sound, are fallible. His is the only voice to reach infinitely above human wisdom.

Jesus' primary mission was to redeem humanity. He was born to die as the perfect sacrifice. For more than three years, however, He also taught about love, people, and morality. In some teachings, He is two millennia ahead of what psychology is coming to understand. In others, He contradicts what psychology preaches.

So, whom to listen to? Well, if Jesus is God ...

2

An IQ Too High

I thank thee, Father, Lord of heaven and earth,
that thou hast hidden these things from the wise
and understanding and revealed them to babes.

—Matthew 11:25

Ask someone: What is IQ? Most people would answer with something along the lines of, "It's how smart you are." What do the letters "IQ" stand for? Some would know that "I" stands for *intelligence*. Fewer would know that "Q" is *quotient*. IQ is the abbreviation psychologists give to someone's score on an "intelligence" test.

Does IQ measure intelligence? Yes and no. (Don't you just love psychologists?) Yes, in that it is a measure of performance compared to others at solving problems mostly related to thinking and reasoning. No, in that such problems are only one piece of what could be called whole intelligence.

Since the early days of intelligence tests, psychologists have gotten smarter about intelligence. Some talk of "social intelligence," that is, the skill at reading others and situations. Some talk of emotional intelligence, the ability to regulate one's emotions. Still others focus on specific talents—musical, artistic, and mechanical, as examples.

An Einstein-like, off-the-scale brilliant nuclear physicist may only have seventh-grade social skills, thus he is tagged with the stereotype "eccentric genius." Conversely, someone who academically barely treaded water may grow up to be a business guru. Some who scored average (or at the fiftieth percentile) on an IQ test might play at the top one percent of gifted musicians.

"Smart" is a far-reaching word. It begs the question: Smart in what way? If asked if they would like to be smarter, very few would answer, "No, I'm good. I have more IQ points than I need, thank you." Most people would grab as many IQ points as possible, though grabbing too many can have a downside, as we shall see.

Whatever it may mean, "smart" is a highly-esteemed trait. Smart and talented people are held to be a cut above the crowd. They are the winners in life's lottery of nature and nurture. "Smart" comes with a whole list of positives.

Why, then, would Jesus, infinitely smart, thank His Father for "hiding these things" from the smart people of His day? It sounds counter-intuitive. The smarter one is, the better able one is to fathom truth. Instead, those "understanding" were not understanding. They were confused.

Some Bible translations use the word "learned" instead of "understanding." "Learned" can have a negative tinge. One can be so settled in his learning that he resists any new learning. He already has everything figured out, so there's no need to ask questions or seek correction. The religious leaders were quite convinced that they had God all figured out, so they didn't want to hear any other insight, particularly one coming from the "unlearned" Jesus.

Jesus challenged them with what psychologists call a "paradigm shift," a different way to look at old information. New wine needs new wineskins. But they refused to listen, because their paradigm had already been set in concrete in their minds.

Have you spoken to others about Jesus? Notice that the more solid they think their reasoning, the less open they are to anyone else's reasoning. On the other hand, a willingness to hear about Jesus shows a curious mind, somewhat like an infant's.

"Experts" of any sort—scientists, physicians, psychologists—often know little to nothing about God or His Son. Expertise in their field, they think, brings expertise in religion. "I'm smart here, so I must be smart over there, too." Their professional knowledge may be at graduate school, but their religious knowledge is still in preschool.

On the other hand, those who seek to know what they can about God don't naturally assume they therefore have expertise in, say, biology or astronomy. Yet those well-versed in biology or astronomy often assume themselves to be well-versed about God. The saying fits them well: "None hold an opinion so strongly as the uninformed."

"Advanced" education makes so many people question Jesus, the Bible, religion, and church. The illogical leap is, "I have questions; therefore, faith is questionable." To quote St. John Cardinal Newman, a brilliant and high-profile Catholic convert of the nineteenth century, "Ten thousand difficulties do not make one doubt."[3] Meaning, questions don't have to nurture skepticism; they can instead nurture answers.

As I wandered away from the Catholic Church, I, too, was grappling with far more questions than I had answers for. "I don't understand" was threatening to sink my faith. Fortunately for me, I couldn't live in a religious limbo about matters with potentially infinite consequences. So, I looked to others smarter and more

[3] *Apologia*, chap. 5 (1852).

informed than myself. Listening to learn what I didn't know brought me back to my childhood faith, with a more adult-like perspective. First, however, I had to assume the role of a student.

Were God to take an IQ test, He'd score perfectly, taking zero time to do so. Not only did He create every skill that can ever be measured, but He knows every test answer in advance.

Measured against God's IQ, mine falls well below that of an infant's. As long as I'm smart enough to know that, then God is ready to teach me. But if I declare sufficient my insufficient understanding, then I am able to block God from lifting me over my self-imposed ceiling.

Jesus linked "wise" with "understanding." "Wise" is more esteemed than "smart." It connotes knowledge and experience used for good.

So again, why would Jesus thank His Father for "hiding these things from the wise"? Perhaps, the answer lies in what is unspoken: "in their own eyes." While wisdom is revered, self-asserted wisdom is not. It is faux wisdom. It calls to mind St. Augustine's lament for having too much faith in one's own knowledge, "Without you [God], what am I to myself but a guide to my own self-destruction?"[4]

Many of those challenging Jesus wrapped themselves in self-anointed wisdom. They were only the wise ones because they said so. Jesus corrected them by speaking to His Father so they could hear. Their very "wisdom" made them less wise than infants. It misinformed them. Until they had authentic wisdom, they would remain foolish.

Jesus wants us to be as children in hearing Him. It is the most intelligent way to be. To raise your spiritual IQ, listen and learn with the humility and openness of a little one.

---

[4] *Confessions*, bk. 4.

3

Unworthy of Self-Worth?

So you also, when you have done all
that is commanded you, say,
"We are unworthy servants."

—Luke 17:10

What grade would Jesus receive in a college counseling class to-day? Would He even pass? To counsel someone to call himself an "unworthy servant" would be asking for an *F*, as it would collide headlong into the prevailing self-esteem gospel.

Another Bible translation gives Jesus' words even more force: "worthless servants." That label would summarily deposit someone at the lowest end of the self-image continuum.

In Jesus' day, there was no self-esteem dogma as celebrated to-day. Only a few decades old, it was birthed in the latter twentieth century in upper academia. Since then, it has thoroughly penetrated the cultural consciousness. No surprise, as it nurtures a universal yearning to regard oneself highly.

Thinking oneself wonderful, it is assumed, is vital to a settled psyche. Indeed, a word once reserved to image God—"awesome"—is now used to image us as well, not to mention chicken sandwiches. Furthermore, an expanding litany of dividends supposedly follows an *awesome* sense of self: achievements, status, inner peace, better hair days. Conversely, as self-esteem slips, personal distress surges—anxiety, insecurity, unhappiness. In short, lift the self-image, and good stuff follows.

With so many positives promoted by so many worldly sages, who would dare question the value of a soaring self-image? Why would Jesus, all-knowing about the human condition, even question it? Talk about angling for a poor grade in counseling class.

Jesus' perspective on self-esteem was two thousand years ahead of what psychology is re-thinking. Modern doctrine may sound uplifting, but real life has left it floundering. At the risk of demeaning self-esteem, it isn't related to much in the way of personal and social well-being.

Even worse, chasing self-esteem for its own sake can lead to some un-Christ-like "selfs"—self-centeredness, self-absorption, self-seeking—all of which stunt virtues like humility, modesty, and empathy. Unbridled self-esteem naturally morphs into self-focus.

What did Jesus mean by "unworthy servants"? In that social hierarchy, servants occupied the bottom layers. They garnered little esteem from themselves or from others. Theirs was a single duty: obey. Hardly a path to a flourishing self-view.

Did Jesus really intend to call His followers society's inferiors? Not in the least. Elsewhere and often, He stresses the inestimable worth of all His Father's children as adopted sons and daughters. "Even the hairs of your head are all numbered" (Luke 12:7). Jesus never questions the infinite value of a person.

Why, then, does He use such striking language? To underscore His words. Routinely, Jesus engages in hyperbole, such as, "And if your right hand causes you to sin, cut it off and throw it away" (Matthew 5:30). Potent counsel demands potent language.

His counsel: When you do what is expected of you, do not expect approval. Don't seek praise when acting praiseworthy. Be dutiful with doing your duty. That is your reward.

The modern mindset says otherwise: Achievements and victories deserve accolades and applause. Jesus disagrees. To translate Him into modern jargon: Don't expect a star on your chart or a participation trophy for acting right.

If you're raising an admirable child, don't broadcast your success to everyone else. If you're financially well-off, don't feel superior to those who aren't. Whatever your accomplishments, be slow to speak of them, if at all.

Whoever you are, whatever you possess, however well others may think of you, know that it all originates from above. God gives and He sustains. The faithful servant never forgets this.

To teach good, or couched in trendy value-neutral language, "appropriate" behavior, psychologists tout using tangible incentives to children — stickers, tokens, money.

Suppose a parent wants her preschooler to learn to make her bed each morning. She searches the internet for "sticker charts for bed-making success," and taping the top-rated chart to the refrigerator door, she follows its formula: Award stickers initially for every bed-making attempt, and once the habit develops, start tapering the stickers, as Dawn is now motivated to make her bed without yellow smiley faces.

That's how it's supposed to unfold, anyway. Some studies, however, assert that as material rewards fade, so does the motivation. Once the carrot is withdrawn, cooperation slips.

Jesus knew. Doing what one ought to do doesn't need to be sustained by stickers, rewards, or recognition. However much appreciated, they are not to be the prime movers of virtuous conduct. Moral actions become ingrained when pursued for themselves.

Does a robust self-image undercut virtue? Not necessarily. A robust self-image, though, is shaped by who makes the call. If Ray

Guarendi declares that Ray Guarendi is a super guy, mine is a plainly subjective judgment. What's to say that I'm all that accurate? After all, my self-image is tied to self-interest. As such, it is built on sand, to rise or fall with my emotions or circumstances. It is too unstable to fulfill all the promises made in its name.

On the other hand, if my Creator, the God of the Universe, declares my worth and my self-image as unassailable, then it is transcendent, as it does not rest upon anything I've done or will do. Whether I consider myself a *wunderkind* or a worm does not alter God's judgment. The call is His, and He has made it unconditionally in my favor.

Psychologists talk of "cognitive dissonance," the holding in one's mind of two apparently conflicting ideas simultaneously. Being an "unworthy servant," yet one with infinite self-worth, would seem to create cognitive dissonance. How can both be true?

In fact, they are both true. They complement one another. An unworthy servant is not a worthless human being. On the contrary, Jesus says He is the one Who serves worthily.

Being a worthless servant is the path to being a worthy disciple.

4

Humility Is Reality

For every one who exalts himself will be humbled,
and he who humbles himself will be exalted.

—Luke 14:11

Jesus not only knew *what* to teach, He knew *how* to teach. He made His words penetrate the heart and settle there.

Advertising pros prize the power of pithy. They concoct catchy slogans to condense their pitch. "Where's the beef?"—a decades-old ad classic that can still conjure up the image of a feisty elderly lady at a fast-food counter. Long before the swarm of Madison Avenue gurus, Jesus was condensing maximum truths into mini packages.

Psychologists like to learn how people learn. They analyze those who teach—who does what well. They know, for example, that information is faster mastered when presented in a familiar format. Thus, lyrics to songs heard in high school can reverberate in the head past social security. Their rhythm and rhyme boost recall.

"On old Olympus temple-top, a fox and gazelle vaulted a hedge" —a ditty from my sophomore biology teacher for learning the twelve cranial nerves. Memory coaches dub this a "mnemonic device." It's a shorthand technique to assist memory. Here, the initial letters of the lyric's twelve words are the same as the initial letters of the twelve cranial nerves.

As you can see, I not only remember the ditty, but I also remember the cranial nerves—well, some of them, anyway. There has been a bit of memory slippage since I was sixteen.

Jesus used His own memory aid: paradoxical phrasing. "For every one who exalts himself will be humbled, and he who humbles himself will be exalted" (Luke 14:11); "For whoever would save his life will lose it, and whoever loses his life for my sake will find it" (Matthew 16:25); "Judge not, that you be not judged" (Matthew 7:1); For if you forgive men their trespasses, your Heavenly Father also will forgive you" (Matthew 6:14).

The second half mirrors the first, making the whole more memorable. Thus, two thousand years from their origin, Jesus' words are easy to quote. He formed them to be so.

What does "He who humbles himself" mean? Does it mean denying one's talents or achievements? Is it a reluctance to accept notice or applause? Is it a self-demeaning personality?

It means: Don't evaluate yourself above others. Nothing of, "I walk among the religious elite; I stand up righteous; I could model for a holiness 'after' picture."

Jesus isn't saying to not seek holiness. He is saying don't seek holiness as religious prestige. Yes, we are exalted by God, as we are made in His image. No, we are not to do our own exalting.

Whom did Jesus most sharply rebuke? Not society's identified sinners, but society's sanctimonious—the religious leaders, those who looked down upon others as the unlearned rabble.

He didn't so much challenge their teachings, but the self-serving attitude wrapped around those teachings. He insisted: Put yourselves into a deferential relationship with God and into an equal relationship with others. Otherwise, My Father will do it for you.

I once attended a weekly Bible study where a question recurred: Why are others so irked by us Christians, especially by our moral principles? A recurrent answer: Our principles convict them. Somewhere flickering inside them is a light telling them what is right.

It's a given: The more closely one walks with Christ, the more he will be misunderstood, particularly by those who want little or nothing to do with Christ. Still, that answer raised a more unsettling question for me. Is it my virtue that rankles others, or could it be something less virtuous? Do I come across as holy, or as holier-than-thou?

Am I being holy or a jerk?

Being a jerk, with or without words, conveys, "You don't have the light that I do" or "I'm not the lost soul you are." Even the promise, "I'll pray for you" can provoke unexpected hostility if it comes with an unspoken, "You do need my prayers to shape up, you know." When offered with condescension, it can come across as a moral put-down.

Fair or not, others will be quick to comment if our march doesn't match our mouth. "Is that how a Christian talks?" "I thought you were the religious one?" "And she claims to be a good Catholic!"

The second car stopped at a traffic signal is adorned with bumper stickers: "My boss is a Jewish carpenter; God is my co-pilot; Know Jesus, Know Peace, No Jesus, No Peace." The signal turns green, and the first car just sits there. Not two seconds later, the second driver lays on his horn and glares ahead with a "Get moving, idiot" face. At the next green, the first car remains idling, as the driver looks to be laughing on the phone. Fuming even hotter, the second driver, now hammering his steering wheel, head stretching out the driver-side window, curses and screams.

Third car in line is a police cruiser, the officer witnessing the unfolding scene. Roof lights flash, and he approaches the raving driver's window. "Please pull over. I'll be right back," he says.

"What?! Why?!" the second driver protests. "You can't pull me over for screaming in my own car!"

"I'm not," replies the officer. "I'm going to run your ID and plates. I want to make sure you didn't steal this car from a Christian."

Does being humbled lead to being humble? Not always. But it is a personal jolt, one which can serve to nudge you toward true humility. Again, humility is not seeing oneself as a lowly worm or, as a rebellious priest centuries ago christened Christians, "dung hills covered with snow."[5]

Neither is it swatting away compliments with reflexive self-deprecation: "I really don't deserve that; I'm not the person you think I am: If only you knew me better." Humility is not thinking less of oneself; it is thinking of oneself less.

Contrary to common thinking, humility is not related to insecurity, a nagging sense that "I'm just not as good or competent as others" in piety, parenting, people skills, or pinochle. Insecurity pushes me to measure myself by the crowd. Rather than being companions, humility and insecurity are opponents. Where humility rules, insecurity doesn't.

Humility is nothing I can profess. "I try to be modest." "You've probably noticed I don't like talking about myself." "I think it's really important to be as humble as I can." A public figure in an interview actually once said, "My humility is something I'm proud of." I've toyed with the idea of writing a book on humility titled *The Three Most Humble People I Know, and How I Taught the Other Two.*

Humility is reality. It is awareness of one's weaknesses, failures, and sins. It is also awareness of one's strengths, successes, and faith-guided obedience. It is not prideful to take delight in obeying God. It is prideful to be self-satisfied in doing so.

---

[5] Attributed to Martin Luther.

Humility is gratitude. Whatever I'm able to do, whatever I possess — talents, wealth, achievements — all come from God. If I credit myself for my gifts, I neglect their Giver. Gratitude crushes pride.

A colleague observed, "It's hard to be self-focused when you're grateful." Being other-focused will take its place.

A young man very much looked forward to visiting his elderly aunt. Rather than saying, "I'm too busy to hang around with old folks," he instead delighted in visiting her. With each visit, after serving the customary drinks and snacks, she settled into rapt interest, bordering on fascination, encouraging him in her easygoing way to talk freely. As he put it, "My aunt wasn't satisfied with the big picture, she wanted the details, the bits and pieces."

Most people around us don't need us to give them food, shelter, or money. What we can give them is a pleasant personality. Few gifts are more appealing than a genuine, other-focused persona.

Jesus wants to give the gift of a humble spirit. He doesn't want us to revel in it, saying, "Thank you, Lord, that with each passing day, you're making me humbler." Humility is the one virtue that if you think you have it, you don't.

Tricky stuff, this humility.

5

Childlike, Not Childish

Whoever humbles himself like this child,
he is greatest in the kingdom of heaven.

—Matthew 18:4

Humble oneself to be the greatest. The contrast is deliberate. Heaven's ideals routinely oppose the world's.

Jesus puts a face to humility with models—servants, those on the bottom rung of the social ladder, and children, one rung up.

Why point to a child? What makes little people good models for big people? After all, they're less morally mature than grown-ups (not always), less rational (not always), and more impulsive (again, not always). Neither are they self-sufficient or well-educated. Some aren't even potty trained.

Is childlike humility simpleminded, naïve at discerning right from wrong, good from bad? Not at all, as Jesus strongly preaches the need for sound moral judgment. Be as wise as serpents" (Matthew 10:16).

How about childlike *honesty?* "You're really old, Uncle Rusty." "Your big legs must make it hard to walk, huh, Grandma?" "I can tell how old you are, Mommy, by counting your wrinkles."

This isn't honesty. It's an unfiltered "what's in my head comes out my mouth." Definitely not a likeable trait for someone young or old.

What does Jesus mean by humbling oneself? What qualities of juveniles—not juvenile qualities—would make someone greater in the eyes of Heaven?

Humility. Humility is born with kids. It's not a virtue they have to earnestly pursue once they can talk. Granted, kids are also born self-centered, but any sense of "I'm superior to you" is not present for years. Single-digit age acts as a hold on grasping for the upper hand.

I know, tell that to a parent standing shell-shocked next to little Will's temper tantrum as he howls, "Do what I want, or else!" However fury-filled, kids still lack the potential to push their druthers upon others, unless of course, adults hand it to them. Their ego is checked by their years.

Forgiving. Children forgive faster and easier than do grown-ups. While they may boil quickly, they cool just as quickly. Puzzled parents observe, "She can be mad at us one minute, and the next she's singing and telling us how much she loves us like nothing ever happened." It's a split-second transformation from Mr. Hyde to Dr. Jekyll.

Feeling aggrieved has a limited life span with kids. Mentally rehearsing transgressions in minute detail takes sophistication they don't yet have. To do so takes adult-like talent, if that's the right word for it. Neither do kids brood for hours or days—years?—over who said or did what to them, and when, where, how much, and with what intent. The adage "forgive and forget" is an operating ethic for most kids.

Not too many kids who are now adults cling to, "I'll never forget how snotty my friend was to me on our first day in kindergarten. It's as fresh now as it was then." How old are you? "Forty-three."

Children don't stand ready to take offense. They don't regress into personalizing—interpreting someone's words or actions as a direct assault on them as a person. Slower to impugn someone's motives, they are quicker to give the benefit of the doubt. Would that my radar for offense be as jammed as theirs.

Dependent. Children enter the world one hundred percent dependent. And they more or less remain so for years, sometimes well into their twenties, but that's a topic for another book. They have no choice but to rely on the god-like beings surrounding them to sustain them. To grow and flourish, they must cling tightly to their caretakers.

Couldn't too much dependence for too long be unhealthy? Shouldn't it be an interim stop on one's way to maturity? That depends—I'm trained to be precise. Upon whom does the dependence rest? If the dependence rests upon someone who is all-loving and all-wise, then it's best never to be outgrown. Jesus is asking for our lifelong dependence upon Him.

Healthy dependence relies on trust. Children are naturally inclined to trust that those watching over them will act in their best interests. Who is unquestionably more trustworthy than God, toward all ages and in all ages? The most loving parents are fallible with imperfect long-range vision. God is infallible with perfect long-range vision. He sees the whole picture from start to finish. We only see bits and pieces.

Our son, Andrew, required several surgeries from infancy to age nine. At age two, to prepare for surgery, he needed his blood drawn. A two-year-old's veins can be buried so deep as to be nearly invisible. As the nurse probed with the needle, Andrew screamed and torqued his little body, trying to escape the pain. I asked her, "Would it help if I held him for you?" As I firmly pinned Andrew's arms down while she searched for the veins, Andrew looked at me, betrayed, as if to plead, "Daddy, I can't believe you are helping them hurt me!" I recall thinking, "Andrew, if you only knew what I know, you'd trust me." During our frequent moments of adult shortsightedness, how often does God think, "If you only knew what I know ..."

Resilience. Childrearing "experts" have done much to frighten parents, warning them of all the potential ways to scar their children psychologically. No surprise, then, many moms and dads tread tentatively, anxious that psychic ferment—seen and unseen—is but one misstep away.

For some time, this perspective has besieged parents. Thankfully, it's finally losing its grip. "Resiliency research" asks the question: How is it that some children not only survive tragic and ugly circumstances but rise above them? Wouldn't some degree of psychic damage be a given?

The potential to repair and recover—psychological plasticity—is greater in the young than formerly thought. Less like emotional spun glass, kids are more like hard rubber wrapped in steel belts. They are built durable. It's God's protective design.

When I was fourteen, my five-month-old brother, Anthony, died of a heart malfunction. I watched it rock my parents' world. While mine, too, was shaken, I returned to "normal" much sooner than they did. Was I repressing my grief? Was I caught up in the self-absorption of adolescence? Not too much, I hope. Looking back, my recovery seemed actually quickened by adolescence, with its zest and high-octane energy. My parents eventually recovered their zest, too, but more gradually than I. Kids are less prone to be emotionally blue and more prone to be upbeat. The Lord wants people of like spirit.

Fifteen months after Anthony's passing, my brother, Mike, was born. Despite our age gap, Mike soon became my best buddy and still is to this day. God has a way of bringing healing from heartache. Childlike trust knows this.

To close the story, after my first son was born, I more fully understood what my parents lived through. It wasn't due to unresolved grief finally surfacing. It was insight born with parenthood.

Jesus is plain: Learn from the children. They can teach us much. Strive to be childlike in the most mature sense of the word.

6

Seek to Be Meek

Blessed are the meek,
for they shall inherit the earth.

—Matthew 5:5

Picture yourself towering over a teeming ant hill with legions of ants skittering in what appears to be random motion. What's their purpose? How are they spending their short-lived existence?

Picture me standing beside you, pointing down and saying, "See that ant hoisting that stick ten times his size? He's the strongest one down there. The one with the huge head next to him is the brains of the bunch. He's far smarter than all the others. But the colony ruler is over there. He runs the whole hill. All the other ants honor him."

Putting aside the question of how I know all about these ants, would you be impressed? Not with me, but with the ants? Probably not. Why not?

Because they're ants. You so transcend them in strength, brains, and everything else, that each ant's hill ranking is meaningless to you.

Jesus, The Master Psychologist

As far as we are above ants, God is immeasurably further above us. The chasm between us and ants is infinitesimal compared to the chasm between us and God.

The most brilliant scientist, the wealthiest tycoon, or the most idolized pop star may hold high status in human eyes, but not in God's. Worldly laurels mean nothing to God. He isn't the least bit impressed by them, no matter their number or how esteemed someone is by how many others.

Julius Caesar can't jump Heaven's line because he was revered as a divine ruler of a powerful far-flung empire. Whoever enters Heaven will do so because of his love for God and others, not because of his fame and adulation. God decrees what makes a life praiseworthy, not name recognition, polls, or number of Twitter followers.

Should earthly honors be gathered as fruits of a faith-filled life, this is not to say they are still meaningless. Rather, Jesus is adamant: These are not to be your priority. Don't pursue them above all else. And never bask in them. They will do little but distance you from walking with Jesus.

"Meek" is not a revered word in our lexicon. Most therapists regard it as a sign of a constricted personality. The thesaurus lists it along with passive, timid, submissive, and doormat. Meek is considered the polar opposite of self-assurance. Who would want to be this definition of meek?

Jesus defines meek altogether differently. To Him, meekness is a noble trait. To be meek is to have no need to elbow oneself past others or to stand above them. Meekness, says Jesus, seeks no praise from others. It doesn't need kudos to feel worthwhile.

Meekness and self-confidence are not competing traits. Rather, they complement each other well. When formed by Christ, they flourish side by side.

If others can coerce me into yielding my principles because I am "meek weak," then my self-confidence, if present at all, will be shaky. To cooperate with others' notions of meekness is to identify with the synonyms in the thesaurus.

Some decades back, a quasi-therapy called "assertiveness training" spread from the minds of academics into the broader cultural mind. It spurred a spate of wildly popular books (*Looking Out for #1*).[6] Assertiveness training claims to be a prescription for those too meek to stand up for their "rights." Whichever of my rights are being trampled, I have a duty to correct the offender. Neglecting this, I risk courting resentment, or worse, becoming a social nonentity.

Shriveling up under social pressure can, without question, breed discontent. An edgy assertiveness, however, can breed even more discontent. To assume a heightened state of vigilance to offense is exhausting, both emotionally and physically. It leaves little room for confident meekness, one that says, "I don't need to set everybody straight each time I feel shortchanged in my due respect."

An untamed assertiveness can be a fierce animal to bridle. If given a long leash, it can be trained into social ugliness. By teaching no one ever to walk on me, I risk teaching them to either walk way around me or to walk far away from me.

Meekness keeps assertiveness balanced. To be meek is to react with little or no agitation to words or conduct that once held the potential to roil me for hours, days even. Meekness is mental vigor.

The link between status and serenity is erratic at best, so tells the lives of countless celebrities. Accumulating brass rings doesn't fill an existence. It too often empties it. In the words of a plaintive song, "Is that all there is?"

Ravi Zacharias, a late Christian speaker, notes, "Pleasure without God, without the sacred boundaries, will actually leave you emptier than before. And this is biblical truth, this is experimental [*sic*]

---

[6] Robert Ringer, Funk and Wagnalls, 1977.

truth. The loneliest people in the world are amongst the wealthiest and most famous who found no boundaries within which to live. That is a fact I've seen again and again."[7]

Ignoring voices like Ravi's, society asserts: Seek recognition. It is the path to fulfillment.

Jesus pushes back: Seek to be meek, not in a passive, pushover way — He certainly wasn't — but in a contented way, the better way, head-wise and soul-wise.

"Blessed are the meek." Meekness doesn't choose power, place, or prestige. All are fragile and fleeting. And in the end, they come to nothing. Worse, they may be the very quests that forsake Heaven, or in other words, prevent one from inheriting the earth.

[7] Twitter.com.

7

Cui Bono?

"How often shall my brother sin against me,
and I forgive him? As many as seven times?"
Jesus said to him, "I do not say to you
seven times, but seventy times seven."

—Matthew 18:21–22

If you never took Latin or did but can't remember much more than
E pluribus unum, Cui bono means "Who benefits?"

"Three strikes and you're out!"—a credo of criminal justice.
If one is convicted of a third serious offense, the penalty is long-
term incarceration. No more chances after sinning against others
three times.

The religious leaders who quarreled with Jesus preached likewise. Sin against another three times, and you forfeit receiving
mercy.

Peter knew that Jesus preached to show more mercy than did
those setting the religious rules. So, he asked Him, "How many
times should I forgive my brother? Seven times?" He probably felt
pretty good about more than doubling the threefold limit.

Jesus, The Master Psychologist

Jesus answered Peter by rocketing the number skyward. "Not seven, but seventy times seven." Is four hundred ninety a literal quota? After reaching it, is one's mercy obligation finally met? In some testy relationships, four hundred ninety could be reached within months, maybe even weeks. Jesus put no numerical ceiling on forgiveness. He meant to forgive always and completely.

Who can forgive always and completely? On our own, that would be a demanding stretch, if not an impossible one. But with God's inexhaustible help, we can reach upward toward it. Even for those who don't listen to Jesus, the stretch is still worthwhile. *Cui bono?*

The consensus is that the one forgiven benefits more, as she receives clemency and kindness. Indeed she does, but the forgiver benefits more and longer.

Clinging to "I've been wronged"—who wouldn't if this were done to him?—imprisons the clinger. The wrongdoer may have no inkling of her offense or even believe she did anything wrong or care that I'm hurting. I'm the one who is emotionally roiled. I desperately need her to know what she did and be sorry for it.

What if she sees no reason to be sorry? In her eyes, the problem is me. That she sees it this way is not all that surprising. More often than not, we think someone needs our forgiveness more than he does.

Were you to offer a sincere "I forgive you," you could receive a perplexed look: "For what?"—or you could be rebuked. You impugned her innocence, much like an "I'll pray for you" might provoke a "How dare you!" rather than a "Thank you." Just because you forgive doesn't guarantee you'll be forgiven for forgiving.

Whether or not someone accepts forgiveness is—forgive me—irrelevant. To bind my willingness to forgive to another's willingness to be forgiven is risky. It puts my peace into her hands. My soul won't be soothed unless she decides to cooperate. I'm left to hope she comes around to my way of thinking.

Refusing to forgive carries with it no shortage of ill emotional and spiritual effects—agitation, resentment, vengeance, and depression, to name a few. I, not the one who hurt me, am punished more by it. Someone somewhere said, "Holding on to ill will toward another is like ingesting a little bit of poison every day and waiting for that other person to get sick."

Reasonable parents know that reason, no matter how compelling, can't always replace good discipline—rules backed by consequences. Few kids—I did read once about one in Nova Scotia—when hearing the "why" for good behavior cheerfully concede, "Why, thank you, Mother. You make such total sense. That's why you're the grown-up, and I'm the child. Can we sing 'Give Peace a Chance?'" Uh huh.

Discipline delivers moral direction. Discipline is not "tough love." It *is* love.

One simple form of discipline is the "if-then." An if-then is a logical proposition. It conveys what's expected along with the results of ignoring or rejecting those expectations. It sets conditions.

"Clay, if you track dirt into the house, you'll vacuum every room where you tramped." "Please turn off the TV, Nielson. If I have to turn it off, I decide when it comes back on." "Macy, if you nag me one more time to take you to the mall, my answer will be no."

Like a loving parent, Jesus not only reasons with us, He disciplines us. He lays heavy consequences on refusing to forgive others.

The Lord's Prayer—the perfect prayer—exhorts us to ask our Father to "forgive us our debts, [a]s we also have forgiven our debtors" (Matthew 6:12). We *must* forgive if we want God's forgiveness. It's the if-then.

Jesus follows with, "For if you forgive men their trespasses, your heavenly Father also will forgive you, but if you do not forgive men their trespasses, neither will your heavenly Father forgive your trespasses." Forgiving is not only good; it's a must.

Jesus, The Master Psychologist

A must isn't meant to constrict. It's meant to liberate.

"Seventy times seven." Literal or symbolic, that's a whole lot of forgiving. My pushy brother-in-law, my bossy boss, my prickly neighbor—none will stop with the slings and slights. Is there some way I can lower my obligation to forgive them, say to around thirty-five times seven or 50 percent of the time or maybe even lower?

A scenario: My wife is heading out for the evening. She asks her mother to watch our children, even though I'll be home. What is she saying? That my caregiving is suspect? (The kids need to be fed? When?) Consequently, I confront my wife for making me look inept, as I see it, in front of her mother, no less.

My wife reminds me that I'm child number eleven (no argument from me) and that her initial strategy was to put our ten-year-old daughter in charge. Her full intent, however, was to give me some free time to work on my latest book. Like that's supposed to assuage me.

What just happened? One, I misread my wife's motives. Two, I took offense based upon my misreading. Third, after settling down, I was ready to forgive. And here's the rub: There wasn't anything to forgive. My wife did nothing wrong. Her offense dwelt only in my head. My sense of aggrievement was hanging solidly in emotional midair. As it turns out, this was not a "seventy times seven" occasion.

How often, I wonder, have I labored to overlook an offense, feeling myself pretty magnanimous, when in fact no offense existed? My misinterpretation, my oversensitivity, or my defensiveness convinced me I was "sinned" against. I don't know the total, but I'm sure it's still rising. I do know it's well over four hundred ninety times.

When forgiveness is coming hard, what can move you past your reluctance?

Decide to forgive. "I don't at all *feel* forgiving. I would be fooling myself." Psychologically speaking, it's not always bad to fool oneself. Forgiveness is not linked to the proper feeling. The notion that for forgiveness to be authentic it must "feel right" is complete nonsense. Jesus tells us that forgiveness is an act of obedience. If forgiveness were a feeling, it would be that much harder to muster. Feelings can be durable, resisting reshaping. It is the mind that pushes the will toward forgiveness.

Renounce retaliation. Medicine's first principle is, "Do no harm." The cure must not be worse than the illness. Thus, the wry observation: "The operation was a success, but the patient died." Likewise, forgiveness can't take hold while I'm still itching to fight back.

Pray for your offender. "But I say to you, Love your enemies and pray for those who persecute you" (Matthew 5:44).

What exactly do you pray for? That she wins the lottery? That she sells her home above the asking price? That her kids earn a college scholarship?

To pray for another means to pray for her moral good. For insight. For repentance. For movement toward God.

Prayer is not only good for the prayee, it's good for the prayer. To use motivation lingo, it's a win-win. Brooding over offense fades as I pray for the offender. Prayer and payback are adversaries. Prayer crowds out thoughts of retaliation.

Mentally rehearsing hurts and pondering reprisals is not good for the self or the soul. It provokes a state of unsettledness. It undercuts contentment.

To always and perfectly forgive may be reachable this side of Heaven only by a heroic, saintly few. Nevertheless, it's a reach well-worth every bit of effort it takes for us less saintly types.

8

True Gold

*So whatever you wish that men
would do to you, do so to them.*

—Matthew 7:12

It's the Golden Rule, as it is universally called. For millennia, it's
been revered as the most succinct guide to moral living.

Jesus is its most well-known advocate, though others have
advanced their particular versions, slanted more toward the "don't
do"—what you would not have others do to you, do not do to
them.

As is His way, Jesus raises the standard, promoting the positive:
Do to others as you would have them do to you. His remains the
most oft-quoted version.

The Golden Rule is solid psychology. Most of us know how we
would like to be treated by others. Our preferences are tightly tied
to our self-interest, or as Christianity calls it, our fallen human
nature. The Golden Rule directs us to overcome our fallen nature.
It converts self-interest into other interest.

Jesus, The Master Psychologist

The Golden Rule is to guide my actions toward you, not yours toward me. There is an informal law. Call it the Law of Social Reciprocity: If I treat you well, you should treat me well; that is, you should reciprocate. This law places an asterisk on the Golden Rule: I will do right toward you *if* you do right by me. Jesus allows no ifs. His command is, "Do unto others," not "Do unto others unless ..." Insisting that you treat me as well as I treat you runs headlong into an unyielding reality: I simply can't make you do unto me as I wish you would.

Living my life by the Golden Rule, however, can move others to live better toward me. To receive respect, I'll give respect. To receive kindness, I'll give kindness. To receive forgiveness, I'll give forgiveness. To be heard, I'll listen. There is no guarantee I'll receive in the same measure that I give. Not everyone listens to the Golden Rule. Jesus tells me to listen to it.

Could another misuse my good intentions to further his own self-interests?

The joke is that an elderly farmer is seated in a church service when a vile, sulfur-reeking creature explodes onto the scene. Panicked, people rush blindly toward the doors, leaving only the old farmer, sitting unfazed.

Enraged that he can't terrify this last remaining congregant, the creature ratchets up his menacing.

"Do you know who I am?"

"Yep."

"And you're not scared?"

"Nope."

"Why not?"

"Been living with your sister for forty-five years."

Unless you live with Satan or his sister or one of his cousins, changing yourself for the better is the best way to change another. Even if the Golden Rule is a faint footnote in another's moral code, most people will take kindlier to a kinder you. Your returns may not come in the same proportion you give, nonetheless, receiving some good is better than none, and much better than receiving bad.

Standing on its own, the Golden Rule can wobble. What if "do unto me" is neither healthy nor moral? "I'm into using street drugs. Want to join me?" "I've been viewing pornography for years. Want to see some sites?" "Cheating is the best way to get ahead. Don't you think so?"

When my wishes for me are self-destructive, the Golden Rule is turned inside-out.

What is the greatest commandment? Jesus answered, "You shall love the Lord your God with all your heart, and with all your soul, and with all your mind, and with all your strength." Then He added, "You shall love your neighbor as yourself" (Mark 12:30–31). Jesus anchors the Golden Rule to first loving God. Otherwise, detached from God-spoken truths, the Golden Rule just becomes an umbrella under which I can gather my personal rules, however good or bad.

"Love your neighbor as yourself." What if my neighbor doesn't love himself? "I just don't feel all that loveable," many say. Self-loathing is an epidemic in our society, as evidenced by the escalating rates in depression and suicide.

As the self-esteem tsunami washes over everybody, ironically a sense of inadequacy and unlovability ensnares more souls. Self-love separate from God's never-wavering love is precarious.

Jesus assumes that we love ourselves because we trust in the Father's love. My self-love is grounded in God's love. It is not rooted in the shallow soil of self-declared self-elevation. "I declare myself wonderful, and that is enough to make it so."

If I see me as God sees me, I will see you likewise, however else you may see you.

Jesus, The Master Psychologist

A perverse paraphrase of the Golden Rule is: "He who has the gold rules." Money is power, it is said. Grab and hold tight right now to what you can.

For those who seek eternity, the Golden Rule is far better paraphrased: To live a life of true gold, follow Jesus' investment advice.

9

Mouth Control

Not what goes into the mouth defiles a man,
but what comes out of the mouth.

—Matthew 15:11

As best as I can recall, the last time I peevishly pushed my sister was around age eight. My most recent physical altercation happened sometime during my freshman year in high school. In my twenties, I did throw some elbows during a few pickup basketball games.

Most likely, you, too, have had few, if any, physical scuffles with others. That's just not what civilized people do. Instead, you rely on words to scuffle. My rough estimate is that 99.135% of face-to-face friction happens with the mouth.

If I could get do-overs for all those moments when my mouth had a mind of its own, I'd invite all my family, friends, and anyone else I had targeted to one place (a stadium?) for a mass group apology.

I might try to hide behind: "My emotions were doing the talking." At that, emotions, even those in the red zone, don't override all self-control. I'd be prospecting for excuses. Excuses neutralize apologies.

Jesus, The Master Psychologist

Religious leaders accosting Jesus had crafted a recipe of rules for proper eating protocol. Sloppiness toward their rules, they maintained, led to sloppiness toward God, or worse, to defilement.

Jesus challenged their rules: Sin does not enter a person through what enters his mouth. Sin enters through what exits his mouth, those vile words not muted but spewed unchewed.

There's no question: it's all too human to speak in anger too quickly, against our own good and the good of others. When impulse sabotages judgment, stuff pours forth that should have been left stuffed.

As a therapist, I've seen repeatedly that if heated thoughts were allowed to cool before crystalizing into words, therapy would have far fewer wounds to mend.

A shoe company has a well-heeled slogan: Just do it. Apparently, the slogan moves people, as sales have skyrocketed. It taps into the power of the will. "Just act."

Would the opposite, "Just *don't* do it," wield the same power? How about, "Just don't say it?"

Raw emotions and regrettable words follow a predictable trajectory. Fierce feelings amplify decibel levels. Worse, the closer the words to the peak of emotion, the more likely to be harsh, hurtful, or hostile.

To break the chain, resolve: Stay silent. For twenty seconds —okay, ten—don't say what feels like an overwhelming urge to say. Stare (not glare), sigh (quietly), or look dumb (easier for some of us than others). Study the ceiling, the floor, the dog, the clock. Disconnect your thoughts from your distress. Despite the sense, apex emotions don't last long. The flame cools. Keep quiet during the worst of it, and you'll need less energy to stifle your worst. Silence sounds less foreign the more it substitutes for sounding off.

Granted, a perceived injustice invites stewing, but silence gives emotions time to simmer. Should you later air your thoughts, you'll be more measured, your voice softer. Harsh words, no matter how on-target, are hard for most anyone to hear.

The emotional parallels the physical. Novice weightlifters, with time and effort, can reach a bench press of two hundred pounds or more. Overcoming that much gravity is inconceivable to someone first walking into the gym. He must grab a weight that challenges him but is still possible. With repeat visits, the once unthinkable becomes the doable, and the doable becomes easier.

Holding your tongue (it weighs about four ounces) might seem as Herculean as performing fifty push-ups your first day at the gym. Like any successful weight training, mouth training takes practice and perseverance.

"But what comes out of the mouth proceeds from the heart, and this defiles a man. For out of the heart come evil thoughts, murder, adultery, fornication, theft, false witness, slander. These are what defile a man" (Matthew 15:18–19). Words are the outward testimony of inward desires and temptations. Thoughts lead to words lead to action.

Jesus warned that at the heart's depth, the core of our thinking and our emotions, lies wrongdoing, or what modern therapeutic lexicon has morally whitewashed as "inappropriate" or "unacceptable" choices.

Pulsating ill will or ruminating retribution are not merely "inappropriate." Jesus insists that these are what defile a person, not prohibited foods, though one could argue that some of the fare we consume does defile.

Several decades back, cognitive behavioral therapy entered the counseling scene, rapidly rising to the top. Its main tenet: Not only do events and circumstances impact our well-being, but also how we interpret them. The meaning we give them affects our mood and conduct, for better or for worse.

I consulted at a skilled care rehabilitation center. Debilitating accidents brought young adults to the facility. Their despair varied greatly, largely moved by how they saw the rest of life unfolding: as unfair and effectively over or as an endless series of hurdles to overcome.

A mother of two, call her Pat, came to my office after her husband had left her for a much younger woman, rupturing her once stable world. With his betrayal came her thoughts of suicide. Over a marathon session, we probed her thinking: "I'm scared of single motherhood. I believed our marriage was solid. How will I survive financially? This wasn't how I saw my life going."

As distressing as these worries sounded, they were not the thoughts propelling Pat toward self-destruction. The worst emotional havoc arose from: "I failed as a wife. Why else would he leave me? I've always assumed there was one soulmate for me, and now he's gone. Divorce is wrong. Am I headed for Hell when I die?"

Pat was convinced that, one, she had ruined her past; two, sabotaged her future; and three, risked her eternal destiny — a soul-crushing trio of beliefs. Fortunately, together we were able to challenge and mitigate those beliefs, leaving her still scared and distressed but not paralyzingly so.

"Defile," just like "sin," is a scorned word these days. It speaks too bluntly. Yet it does seem well-suited to capture the full bite of an unbridled mouth.

"Trait talk" — flinging broad accusations at another — is a particularly heavy verbal cudgel. Trait talk sneers, "You are thoughtless," rather than, "That was a thoughtless thing to say." "You are mean," rather than, "That was a mean thing to say." "You are inconsiderate," instead of, "You didn't consider my feelings."

Trait talk is not only vague, it also provokes defensiveness. Should you feel the urge to point out someone's shortcomings — in your judgment, that is — keep it specific. Speak to his behavior, not to his character. In short, don't let your mouth get personal.

The baseball world plays by the maxim "addition by subtraction," which means to strengthen a lineup by cutting off a weak player. This is also a smart strategy for a winning personality. Eliminate words that can ding and damage, and your relationships should strengthen. At a minimum, they won't weaken.

St. James reiterates Jesus: "Look at the ships also; though they are so great and are driven by strong winds, they are guided by a very small rudder wherever the will of the pilot directs. So the tongue is a little member and boasts of great things. How great a forest is set ablaze by a small fire! And the tongue is a fire" (James 3:4–6).

Whether one's words are impulsive or deliberate, they can fracture human connections. The verbal can hit harder than the physical. Getting a grip on one's mouth is a prime aim for the Christian.

Families with children witness "sibling quibbling," or two or more partially socialized, partially moralized human beings grappling while living within hitting distance of one another. Parents ask, "How can I teach my children to treat each other better? They clash constantly." My foolproof suggestion: Allow only one child in the house at a time. Short of that, no other strategies exist to completely eradicate sibling squabbling. However, a first step toward good treatment is to curtail bad treatment. Implement zero tolerance toward name calling, tormenting, and put-downs. Enforce it with discipline, and the relationships should become more familial. Addition by subtraction.

You're presenting the kids with two options. The first: Cease all contact, highly unlikely, given they inhabit the same square footage and breathe the same air. The second: Curtail the bickering. Almost all kids gravitate toward option two, even if not initially so disposed. "Mom, make him stop looking at me."

All relationships—kid to kid, adult to adult—follow the same pattern. When not injured by rough words, they move toward healing.

Control your mouth, Jesus says, and you will control a main opening of sin. A monitored mouth also offers a bonus: You never have to apologize for what you didn't say.

10

Mind Control

But I say to you that every one who
looks at a woman lustfully has already
committed adultery with her in his heart.

—Matthew 5:28

Jesus is absolute: Follow God's design for sexual intimacy. It is for your utmost good, as well as for the good of others. "Don't look lustfully," however, has guidance beyond sexual morality.

One, don't do wrong, even if no one else would know you did it. Two, don't think about what you could get away with if the opportunity arose. Three, if you do the wrong you thought you'd like, you may find out how much you don't like it, or yourself for that matter.

A pastor once instructed his congregation, "If you don't act immorally only because you could get caught, you're not being virtuous. You just may be a coward."

"Okay, but at least I didn't do anything wrong," one might insist. But he wanted to. Obeying Jesus is not what pushed him to act morally. Self-interest did.

"I've been thinking of how I could retaliate." "I can't get over how mad I am." "After what she did, I just want to let her have it." "This whole situation has been bothering me for days, and I'm about ready to explode."

Much sin is born in the head. Sometimes, it remains there. Sometimes, it surges into expression. The mind feeds the heart, and the heart feeds the mouth or the feet.

The longer one entertains doing wrong, the more likely he will do wrong. What percolates inside pushes for expression outside. Brooding over an offense or fantasizing about a forbidden temptation gives it energy. Sinful thoughts are not only wrong in themselves; they carry the seeds of sinful deeds.

Most therapists agree with Jesus, though they might not recognize Him as a mentor. They've learned how powerfully thoughts can provoke or subdue bad behavior.

A scenario: You're crammed with people within a three-sided bus shelter. Unforgiving gusts of wind fling cold, biting raindrops inside as everyone shrinks toward the back wall. Whereupon, what feels to be the sharp point of a closed umbrella starts jabbing your heel. "What is this?" you think. "Someone's idea of fun?" As the jabs continue, so does your irritation. Were I standing next to you, asking, "Why are you getting so upset?" you'd answer, "Because some jerk is playing games with my heel!"

Lurching around to fend off the umbrella-wielding stabber, you come face to face with an elderly blind woman, disoriented by the mass of shifting bodies and using her cane for balance. What happened to your anger? Gone in a nanosecond. Did you have to choke back, "You're lucky that's not an umbrella, lady?" Not at all. Your agitation was not fueled by the heel jabs, although they did hurt. It was fueled by your thoughts about what the jabs meant. When your perception changed, in an instant anger was replaced by contrition and probably some sheepishness. It's a dramatic illustration of how quickly thoughts can alter emotions, for better or for worse.

"Not what goes into the mouth defiles, but what comes out of the mouth" (Matthew 15:11). And what comes out of the mouth quite often starts in the head. To entertain wrongdoing in the head—or heart—gives it sanctuary, a place to remain hidden as it grows. No one else knows it's there, and that's what makes it so insidious. It can metastasize unchallenged until you actively work to expunge it.

"I can't help the way I feel." It may feel so, but that is patently false. Feelings aren't born on their own. They have parents: thoughts. They rise or retreat, depending upon how we read others, situations, and ourselves. Most of what happens to us or around us must be interpreted. And faulty interpretations all too often have a partner: sin.

A second scenario: You're at your mother-in-law's birthday party. At its smoothest, your relationship with her has been edgy. You've sensed she's always believed that her son could have done better in his selection of a mate.

Meandering toward the kitchen for a piece of cake, you overhear her talking with her daughter about you, and it's no litany of your positives.

Staying out of sight (yes, it's sneaky, but the temptation wins), you get an earful. Each criticism raises your emotional temperature by at least three degrees. Your first impulse is to storm in there and vent some of your heat. Instead, you slink back to the family room, seething. Grabbing your husband, you make it clear you want to leave—*now!* Whatever party mood you were in minutes ago has been squashed, perhaps for the next several days. After some hurried "got to go" excuses, backing out of the driveway, your husband braves a "what happened in there?" face. Then he gets an earful, as you link his mother to your distress. She was cold and callous, even for her.

Did she precipitate your agitation, and with it an "I'm going to let her have it" plan? Sort of. What she did was mean and unfeeling. What you were telling yourself about her conduct inflamed your distress even more. Some possibilities: "She has no right to berate me, behind my back and to her daughter, no less. She needs to take a long look at herself first. I've tried so hard to get along with her, and this is my reward. What if my husband makes some flimsy excuse for her, telling me to calm down and to not let her get to me?"

Anyone, anytime, anywhere can act wrongly toward you, whether you deserve it or not. The longer you rehearse the injustice of it all, the more that ill will follows. To check the impulse to shoot off a set-her-straight e-mail twelve seconds after arriving at home, turn your thoughts from her toward you. Specifically, how are you riling yourself up? What are you telling yourself that is pushing you at the least toward mental hostility and at the worst toward active hostility?

An emotion may feel automatic, a reflex reaction to an ugly situation or a provocative person. Despite the feeling, the reaction doesn't happen in isolation. It is the thoughts or desires preceding and sustaining it that can generate heat or calm, right or wrong.

Mental rehearsal invites sin not only into the head and heart but into the life. "Don't lust" says much more than simply "don't lust." It says "don't even think" about sin, no matter what kind. Without the thought, sin is deprived of oxygen. It can't breathe the air of reality.

11

Welcome a Child, Welcome Jesus

Whoever receives one such child
in my name receives me.

—Matthew 18:5

Little people can teach us big people a thing or two about humility, trust, and forgiveness, so says Jesus, more than once. We may outgrow what long ago came more naturally to us only to pump more energy into making it come more naturally again.

In Jesus' day, kids didn't have high status. In fact, they ranked just a little above low-status adults—the poor, the shunned, the handicapped, the "sinners."

To "receive" can mean "to care for." Jesus makes receiving society's lessers, which includes children, so core to His teaching, that He places Himself among them. He knew then what social psychologists know now: Caring for another benefits both the cared for and the caring.

Our thinking about receiving children could be called schizophrenic, or in the literal sense of the term, split-minded. On one hand, we regard children highly. We safeguard their well-being, champion their self-image, and take delight in their abilities, sometimes so much that we will use their abilities to elevate our own status.

On the other hand, while we welcome children, we don't welcome too many. Two per family is the societally acceptable number. You might be granted an exemption for three, if the first two are the same sex. "You'd like a boy, too?" "Trying one last time for your girl?"

Stretch beyond three, however, and the comments multiply per offspring: What are you, irresponsible? (irony) Selfish? (serious irony) Clueless about the birds and the bees? (ultimate irony) No TV in your bedroom? Soaking up more than your fair share of the earth's oxygen?

Our culture has its arms wrapped tightly around a "liberating" carnal code: If it feels good—even if not—do it. Pretty much any sexual pursuits are okay, applauded even. Pretty much any except having more than 1.86 children in marriage.

A ruling sexual commandment: Don't judge anyone's actions, unless she's a married mother of more than three or a pregnant mother already with two or more children. Then she's asking for it.

"Don't you know how this is happening?" Of course. Don't you?

"Do you have a television?" We have three, and the biggest one's in the bedroom.

"Are you going to get fixed?" I didn't know I was broken.

"Are these all your children?" Of course not. The oldest is at home with the triplets.

Much of the world is purposely practicing something that past societies, even those relegating kids to second-class status, couldn't comprehend. During only the past few generations, dozens of "developed" countries have not birthed enough children to replace the adults who are dying. Recently, the U.S. has entered that expanding list.

If demography is destiny, many countries are committing slow demographic suicide. Their days as "developed" are numbered.

More young people talk of, "No kids for us." "I can't see myself with children." Now or never? "I don't think it's good to bring a child into the world at this time." When would be a good time? "There are too many people on the earth." How are you so sure you're not one of the "too many"?

"Our friends have babies and little kids, and they're all wrapped up in them. But we just don't share that kind of excitement." In greater numbers, young couples wonder if they're suited for parenthood. Even so, if they do step past their uncertainty and give birth, their progression from doubt to delight takes, oh, about a day or so. Their once so certain disinterest toward others' "crumb crunchers" crumbles with the arrival of their own. They don't need to read *How to Accept Your Child into Your World.* It happens naturally. Facebook, brace yourself.

If their little Harmony is not the cutest, sweetest, most photogenic kid in the Western Hemisphere, she is, without doubt, in the top ten. Prior to parenthood, most people greatly underestimate how deeply a child can capture their heart. It's a truth bound to biology.

After a child or two, most couples decide, "We're done." I ask, "Did you anticipate how much you'd love your child(ren)?" Not at all. "What makes you think you wouldn't love another child as much?" They admit they would, and if they do venture into the unknown, they always find that love doesn't divide; it multiplies.

Throughout my forty-plus years as a psychologist, I've seldom heard a parent look back and say, "I should have had less kids." Instead, I've heard plenty confess: "I wish I had *more* children." Jesus knows our minds far more intimately than we do. When He advocates a particular path, He knows its rewards.

Although children are souls created by God, this doesn't mean they're souls always easy to live with. For some stretches, they can be downright hard to live with.

They are born bent inward toward the self and outward toward rebellion. G. K. Chesterton, an astute social observer, pointed out: The doctrine of original sin is "the only part of Christian theology which can really be proved."[8] If you doubt that, just absorb a few hours of the news.

Socializing and moralizing one's offspring can take the better part of two decades—sometimes longer, as more young adults linger in the nest. Surprises and emotional jolts, along with sundry annoyances, flare up along the way. How could exasperation not intrude? How could you never scold or yell? How could you not say dumb or regrettable things? How could you not sin?

One parent ruefully confessed, "Before I had children, I saw myself as pretty laid-back. Three kids later, I'm more impatient, argue too much, and have to work harder to control my emotions."

None of this means that a parent isn't gracefully receiving children from God, even if she was once more nurturant when Angela was tiny and cuddly and that feeling waned when the word "teen" made the scene.

It attests to one reality: We are inescapably fallible, peppered with imperfections, whether raising one child or eight. In the end, for most parents, the plusses dwarf the minuses. That doesn't mean that the minuses can't double as near occasions of sin.

One saint, after visiting with her sister and her large brood, is reported to have admitted that she was ready to return to her convent, with its hushed peace and solitude.

Some family "experts" warn ominously: A bigger family means poorer parenting. It invites more conflict, they say. It divides attention. It causes faster aging—okay, I made that one up, but it would depend on the kids.

---

[8] "The Maniac," in *Orthodoxy*.

Some parents concede, "I wanted more kids, but I've changed my mind. My hands are full with the two I have now." They assume another child would dilute their parenting, when in fact it could concentrate it.

One mother said, "I think I'm a better mom of six than I was of two." With each child, she learned what to expect, what was "normal," when to act and when to ignore. She better navigated the ups and downs of raising diverse personalities. The kids forced her into a savvier motherhood.

Never doubt your heart for children by your bouts of ruffled parenting. Jesus wouldn't ask us to welcome these little ones if we weren't capable, with His help, of doing so.

"Receive one such child" has a literal meaning: To care for a child that is not yours by birth. Or to adopt.

Our life expectancy relative to almost all earlier times and places is off the charts. Forty or fifty years of life in Jesus' time was close to the maximum. Consequently, losing one or both parents during one's childhood was not all that uncommon. It was a lingering tragic possibility.

In our day, children lose mother, father, or both less through death but more through deadly habits—a reckless or abusive or addictive or anti-social lifestyle. A disordered life can wound a child in the womb and thereafter. An adoptive parent can give to a child the stability she needs to mature past her rocky beginnings.

St. James echoes Jesus: Pure faith before the Lord is taking care of widows and orphans (James 1:27).

Jesus is not ordering His followers to adopt or to be open to any child from anywhere at any time. His is a call, not a command.

Some parents or hoping-to-be parents do hear the call, but it's muted by their circumstances—age, finances, health, employment, or a spouse who doesn't hear it.

Others want to answer the call but wrestle with assorted questions and anxieties. Will I connect emotionally with this child, and she with me? How will my relatives react? Will this decision disrupt my family life? How much? Can I persevere through any unexpected headaches or heartaches? Those questions and more are addressed in further detail in my book on adoption.[9]

One simple yet profound answer to all such "what ifs?" comes from Mother St. Teresa of Calcutta, who said, "We are called to be faithful, not successful."

My wife's and my adopted children come from completely contrasting backgrounds—some stable, some chaotic. As they are all now young adults, she and I facetiously observe, "Some could serve the Church; some could serve time."

Looking at our family picture, my wife reminds me, "We are not their Savior." Our call was to give them a loving, steady family. Were we to think we couldn't, then adoption wouldn't have been on our radar.

What Jesus asks of us is not marked by our victories but by faithful perseverance. Some parents, whether by giving birth or adopting, watch their child drift away from or outright reject their upbringing. The story, however, is seldom over. In time, these same parents may watch their young adult slowly regain his former Faith and morals. He comes to realize his parents gave him the foundation for a well-lived life. The system works.

"Whoever receives one such child in my name receives me." Meaning, even if one such child is the least in society's eyes, he is not the least in God's eyes. Meaning, children are much more soul-satisfying than the prevailing "wisdom" about family size insists.

---

[9] Excerpt from *Adoption: Choosing It, Living It, Loving It,* by Dr. Ray Guarendi, Franciscan Media, 2009.

Meaning, plenty of children are awaiting a parent to walk with them to adulthood.

Jesus wants our trust in Him to be childlike throughout our entire lives. Put another way, it takes being like a child to receive a child.

12

A Chip off the Old Block

Or how can you say to your brother, "Let me take
the speck out of your eye," when there is the log
in your own eye? You hypocrite, first take the log
out of your own eye, and then you will see clearly
to take the speck out of your brother's eye.

—Matthew 7:4–5

Scottish poet Robert Burns wrote, "Oh, would some Power give us the gift to see ourselves as others see us."[10] That's a gift I'd gladly welcome, as long as others see good in me and not so much if they don't. I take feedback much better when it's positive.

Seeing ourselves as others see us is the axe to chop chunks off our log. As the log splinters, our vision clears.

My log shrinks when I admit it's there. The thickest log is the one I don't see.

---

[10] From his poem, "To A Louse, on Seeing One on a Lady's Bonnet at Church," 1786.

In my defense — a phrase that easily rolls off my tongue, or my log — not all at every time are equally clear-eyed about me. After all, they, too, have their own logs. Their eyesight toward me could be as crisp as 20/20 or as blurred as 20/200.

Whatever their vision, the question for me is: How accurate are they? A little or (shudder) a lot? If a lot, then why have I been so oblivious? Because old logs can become petrified.

Suppose someone jolts me with the accusation: "You're self-centered." (Who, me? What about you?) "Self-centered" is a sweeping and disparaging charge. I'm tempted to reflexively reject it. Instead, what if I seek details? "What do you mean by self-centered?" "How do I come across like that?" "Can you give me some examples?" "Am I self-centered only with you or with everybody?"

Self-introspection through the eyes of another is seldom pleasant. It calls for both humility and confidence — the humility to admit fault, and the confidence not to be personally shaken by hearing it. Criticism stings more if I think I'm a failure.

A major irony. The heaviest accusation is one I readily accept: I'm a sinner. To that, I plead guilty — conditionally, anyway. Just keep the charge generic, please. Don't get too specific.

"You get irritated easily with me." "You're late again. Can't you call?" "You've been yelling at the kids a lot lately."

These are distinct faults which I can counter. "I get irritated because you nag me. I'm only late when something unexpected comes up. If the kids listened better, I wouldn't have to yell so much."

While I say amen to "I'm a sinner," I don't like having my particular sins pointed out. That's cutting a little too close to my everyday sinfulness.

Sigmund Freud is called the father of modern psychiatry. He theorized that psychic conflicts buried deep in childhood must be revealed and unraveled. His therapy — psychoanalysis — was his channel for doing so. "Insight" was his word for bringing unconscious chaos to light.

Psychoanalysis no longer rules the therapeutic scene, but its progeny, talk therapies, also preach insight. Long before the advent of counselors, philosophers urged: Know thyself.

Insight is important to emotional maturity. It's crucial to spiritual maturity. Without it, growth inches upward, if at all. Insight seeks to know: Where do I fall short? How can I do better? What are my motives? Are they obvious or hidden? Do they promote virtue? Do they mesh with Christ-centered conduct?

A nemesis of insight is defensiveness, the impulse to downplay, dispute, or deny. Defensiveness protects. It shields me from hearing what I don't want to hear about me. It is a prime mover of excuses and rationales. It is social jujitsu at black-belt level.

Defensiveness can be subtle. One study compared how we judge others' imperfections with how we judge our own. Mine I tend to attribute to the situation. "Sure, I got mad. But the guy turned right in front of me without using his turn signal." Yours reveal personality flaws. "You got mad after being cut off because you have anger issues." My tolerance for my missteps, moral or otherwise, is greater for me than for you. For me, mercy. For you, justice.

The deepest insights come from God. Though He may not whisper in my ears, "Look at how you're acting," He does share with me His guiding principles. They give me His eyes.

Defensiveness has a prickly relative: offensiveness. It is a hypersensitivity to slights, real or perceived. Offensiveness pervades our culture. College students retreat to "safe spaces," cocooning themselves against anything distasteful to their sense of things. Politicians craft ever-shifting, linguistically correct talking points, so as not to miff potential voters. Teens stand cyber-ready to pummel in kind (unkind?) anyone who circulates anything they regard as "annoying." Be cautious how long you look at someone, lest he feel provoked. "He's looking at me" is no longer a battle cry only for siblings.

"Easy offendability" challenges, "How dare you say that about me!"—or my family, my religion, my haircut. You're not seeing me as I am. Your vision is distorted.

Easy offendability demands recognition, praise, or approval. None of which are due to the follower of Christ. They may be desirable, but they are not social entitlements.

Only one Person deserved no offense or disrespect whatsoever. Only one Person had a flawless personality. Only one Person had not the smallest speck in His eyes. Yet He endured more insults and derision than any of us ever will. Students are not greater than their master.

Psychologists talk about "projection," or observing in another one's own habits or faults. "Can't she see that she does the very same thing she accuses me of?" "'Watch your language,' he says. Does he even hear himself?" "She calls *me* opinionated, why, she's one of the most opinionated people I know!"

Projection is near universal. It is not, however, always a psychological blind spot. Through seeing another, we may better see ourselves.

Suppose I am hyperalert to the sound of someone bragging. My radar can pick it up from two rooms away. Could it be that I, too, tend to turn discussions toward me and my accomplishments?

Anything that remotely resembles gossip pricks my ears. Is this a sign that I have to fight my own bent toward gossip? Does gossip lurk around my next sentence? Whatever I see so clearly in others may be the mirror for me to see in myself.

I asked a priest, "Why is it that the more I want to be like Christ, the more I see where I fall short?" He drew a parallel to approaching a bright light. As I get nearer, the light reveals flaws I had no inkling were present. Christ is the light that enables me to see me more closely. In the short run, that can be discouraging. In the long run, it's encouraging—if I want to be a better person, that is. I'd rather a forty-watt bulb illuminate me. Jesus is a five-hundred-watt LED spotlight.

For Catholics, the Sacrament of Reconciliation, commonly called Confession, has three purposes: To reveal, to repent, and to resolve. For several years, I was apart from the Church and from Confession. My soul-searching was hit and miss, at best. It was easier left undone.

Having returned to the Church and to Confession, I now must regularly probe my moral failings. I can't confess what I don't know to confess. Confession is a high-powered log splitter.

"First take the log out of your own eye, and then you will see clearly to take the speck out of your brother's eye." From whom do you better receive corrective criticism? From one who knows his own warts? Or from one who is unseeing of his but wide-eyed to yours?

Self-awareness fosters good will from others. The better you know you, and the better they know you know you, the better they'll listen when you speak.

Removing a splinter often takes using a magnifying glass. So long as a log covers my eyes, removing the speck in another's is like trying to extract a splinter while wearing sunglasses at dusk. Rather than cleansing his eye, I'm more likely to poke it out.

Jesus and psychology concur: Be ever-ready to look closely at yourself. Absent self-insight, both emotional and spiritual maturity can shudder to a halt. Chip away at the log that blocks your eyes. Better yet, grind it into sawdust. Then dispose of it.

13

Inflated Value

For where your treasure is,
there will your heart be also.

—Luke 12:34

Years ago, a pastor told his congregation, "Show me your check-book, and I'll show you what matters to you." Today, he'd say, "Show me your credit card statement." Either way, the point is made. After meeting the basics, we spend on priorities.

Jesus aimed stern words against showy religious elitism. He spoke just as sternly or even more so against amassing riches, especially when they blind one to others' needs.

Jesus never hesitated to rattle His listeners, to jolt them from their spiritual torpor. Hence the shocker: "It is easier for a camel to go through the eye of a needle than for a rich man to enter the kingdom of God" (Mark 10:25).

How is that possible? Even with a newborn camel and a monster-sized darning needle? Is there a way to make some wiggle room in Jesus' analogy?

Jesus, The Master Psychologist

Some have tried to, by defining "needle's eye." Supposedly, it referred to a door-like entrance in the city's outer wall. Rather than laboriously opening the massive main gates for solo travelers, gatekeepers could allow them to enter along with their animals via the "eye of the needle." But to squeeze through, large beasts had to hunker down and drop their heavy loads.

While a colorful image, scholars question its historical reliability. Jesus may in fact be speaking literally, contrasting a camel's mass with a sewing needle's miniscule eye. Judging by their alarmed question, that's how the disciples understood Him. "Then who can be saved?" To use modern lingo, "What?! Are you saying what I think you're saying?" To use psychology lingo, "I'm hearing you say ..."

Jesus reassures them, and us: "With men this is impossible, but with God all things are possible" (Matthew 19:26). That's a relief. A camel through a door is tight, but doable. A camel passing through a needle's eye is not. As He routinely does, Jesus relies on potent hyperbole to relay a potent message.

Are many possessions in themselves wrong? Does having more stuff equal more sin? It would depend, according to Jesus, upon how much one pursues that stuff and how tightfisted he clings to it. Though St. Paul is routinely misquoted as saying, "Money is the root of all evil," he actually said, "For the *love* of money is the root of all evils" (1 Timothy 6:10). He is recalling Jesus' warning: "No one can serve two masters ... You cannot serve God and mammon" (Matthew 6:24). Only one will gain our higher loyalty.

The good news: We aren't told to shed material comforts to follow Jesus more closely. Jesus did prod the rich young ruler to do so, but Jesus knew the man's many possessions were distracting him from real treasure.

The bad news: Gathering worldly goods can pull us in the same direction as the rich young ruler. It's a gathering littered with snares.

Snare one: "Excess is the norm." Relative to all other times and places, our lifestyles can be summed up in one word: Luxury. Ours is the wealthiest society in history—materially, anyway. The Jewish people in Jesus' time didn't take food as a daily given. Many were unsure of their next calorie intake. Most of us, by contrast, have food in kind and amount that would have astounded not only the Jewish people but their rulers, too. We enjoy so much food, in fact, that obesity is now a major health risk. Stroll along any mega-store's multiple freezer cases, and you can count dozens of assorted ice cream novelties alone.

The typical Palestinian's dwelling could sit inside our garages. Cruise down a residential street, and you can look into garages gorged with enough stock to outfit a small hardware store. One or more cars, being most people's most expensive asset next to their home, are parked outside, unable to squeeze between all the stuff.

Jesus observed that King Solomon in all his regal array couldn't eclipse the beauty of flowers (Matthew 6:28-29). Solomon would also meet his sartorial match in the standard American wardrobe. We replace apparel because it is "out of date," "out of fashion," or simply the wrong color. Torn clothes are the new chic (at the writing of this book), when previously they have always and everywhere been a sign of hardship. We are so well-off that we have to pretend we're not.

Palestinians owned mostly for need and utility. Extras were an extravagance. Jesus spoke out strongly against hoarding possessions at a time when most people couldn't do so even if they wanted to. How much more strongly is He speaking to us today?

Snare two: "More is better." It stifles the serenity which comes with, "I have enough. I don't need more." "My car looks and runs fine, but it is six years old. It's past time for a new upgrade." "If I work longer and harder, I'll be able to live more comfortably one day." One day always seems to be one day away.

Jesus, The Master Psychologist

Richard Swenson, an evangelical Christian, authored a book titled *Margin*.[11] In it, he observes that people push to their absolute limits or above in time, schedule, and money, leaving little flexibility for a more balanced and generous existence. He contends that an over-packed and over-paced lifestyle exhausts and impoverishes. It squeezes out what matters most—seeking God.

Snare three: Accumulation accelerates. The race for more gains speed. My parents were economically middle class. Their house for fifty years—they never spoke about upgrading—totaled somewhere around twelve hundred square feet, average for the time. Modern builders don't routinely offer anything so cramped, as there's little demand for it today. The term "starter home" is no more than a few decades old.

Both our house and car came with air conditioning, open windows. Four siblings shared two bedrooms, one television, and one phone—on a wall, with a cord. *Ewww!* Our TV pulled in four channels, roughly four hundred less than TVs do today. Is it still only four hundred? Or was that last week's menu?

There's no question: technology is driving our every day ever-upward, ever-faster, by the month. The latest and greatest soon becomes a basic, a must-have. To decelerate, must we retreat to yesterday? Should we sell our homes and pitch a tent in the backyard until the new owners evict us? Some of Jesus' followers do forgo much to serve Him better. Most of us, however, live in this world with its increasingly seductive material temptations. Jesus is directing us: Be aware of the pace, slow it down resolutely.

Snare four: The more I own, the more it owns me. It gobbles my time, devours my money, and shortchanges my relationships. My pie isn't limitless. The more I invest in things, the less is left

---

[11] *Margin: Restoring Emotional, Physical, Financial, and Time Reserves to Overloaded Lives*, NavPress, 2004.

to invest in others. Is it a "who" or a "what" that gets my most and best? As Richard Swenson puts it: People, not things.

Jewish law mandated tithing—returning ten percent of one's bounty to God, the giver of all one hundred percent. Jesus upped the percentage, "He who has two coats, let him share with him who has none" (Luke 3:11). That's fifty percent. Is that a literal standard? Rather, it's a guide to counter excessive generosity. I am to give freely to those who have need; that is, if I want "Christ" to be the first syllable of my religious identity.

A priest friend called tithing a sliding scale. Someone who earns $40,000 annually and gives one tenth to church and charity sacrifices more than someone who earns $500,000 annually and tithes $50,000. Both give the same percentage, but the latter still has $450,000 for himself. In households with plenty of money, ten percent might be a better lower limit than an upper one.

Surveys confirm that as a group, those with higher incomes give proportionately less. Why so? One explanation involves seeking security. As wealth accumulates, curiously so does uneasiness about the future. Will I have enough for a well-off retirement, to launch my children financially, or to manage an illness? Having more today can provoke anxiety about tomorrow. Anxiety about tomorrow can rob today of its generosity.

Snare five: More satisfies less. Nothing obeys the law of diminishing returns like materialism. The more I get, the less it pleases me.

Habituation is the adaption over time to what once had an effect. Medications can lose potency as the body tolerates their dose. People adapt to emotional threats that once had the potential to overwhelm them. The body learns how to neutralize microscopic invaders.

Habituation rules over possessions. What once gratified no longer does. What for a time glowed bright now dims. What formerly filled now brings emptiness.

C. S. Lewis, a twentieth-century defender of Christianity, observed in his book *Mere Christianity* that "if we find ourselves with a desire that nothing in this world can satisfy, the most probable explanation is that we were made for another world."

A multi-national survey found that those living in poorer, less-developed countries expressed more contentment than those living in the United States. Why this seemingly upside-down relationship? We have more of most everything identified with the "good life." The answer lies in "have versus want." Dissatisfaction sits in the gap between what we have and what we want to have. The wider the gap, the more discontent with "what is," no matter how much "what is" is. The advertising world makes its money by widening that gap.

If you're feeling the pull of too many possessions, here are some ways to weaken their allure.

One: Eliminate. If something has long sat ignored in a drawer, closet, attic, basement, or car trunk, donate or pitch it. Merely unloading some will weaken the tug of all. How long unseen or untouched renders something expendable? One rule: The more of anything, the sooner some of it can go.

Can I assume you're reading right now? (I'm a highly trained observer.) Can I also assume you like books and that your home library has a good number of them? Some you've never read. Some are left unread. Some you'd like to read again. Some are good for reference. Some touched you.

Several organizations crave solid religious and spiritual materials to forward to seminaries worldwide. Ask yourself: Where will some of my books do the most good? Perched passively on my shelves for years, or actively shaping the minds of those serving God's people?

Initially, "thinning," as my wife calls it, may feel foreign. With practice, it will feel more natural, more rewarding. What for so long you could never let go prompts two questions: Why again do I need this? Does someone else need it more?

Living alongside a pile of possessions can become a comfortable status quo. With each year, the pile never shrinks. Instead, it grows like an untreated mold. Nothing less than a conscious effort can slow its invasion. A yard sale every few years won't do it. Even an annual yard sale might not be enough to thin out all that has crept in from the prior year.

Two: Divide, don't multiply. Do I really need nine hammers, twelve screwdrivers, fourteen paintbrushes and rollers, and seven yard rakes? How about sixteen sweaters, fourteen hats, nine hoodies, and twenty-two pairs of shoes? I could slash half my inventory and still have multiples of just about everything. The Lord's admonition rings in my ears: "Give to him who has none."

Three: Include the kids. Not to be discarded, but to help discard. We own, we insist, because we've earned it. The kids own, too, but only because we earned it. Our gains flow to them. We live well, so they live well. A guide for us to guide them: How much is enough?

A better question: How much is good for them?

Dolly has twenty-nine stuffed animals burying her bed. Cut the menagerie in half, giving to children's charities, and she still has fifteen (kids round up). Either free some animals from the zoo or get Dolly a bigger bed. Would one bed be enough?

Should Mac really collect a trinket toy each and every time he orders a kids' fast-food meal? Isn't choosing from a long list of food choices sufficient? Does he need a reward even though you paid for it?

My daughter Hannah "earned" forty-nine erasers in her first few months of first grade. After completing assignments, each student could grab a prize from the goodie bag. Hannah must have wanted to set the class record for most erasers, because that's all she grabbed. Why stop at forty-nine? Because we stopped her. When we heard of the total (a brother attended the same school) we presented our plan: Pick two favorites and return the rest to the bag. In response, did Hannah start to shirk assignments? No. Her reward shifted from accumulation to achievement. We never found out what Hannah's teacher thought of our plan. We did hear what Hannah thought, not forty-nine times, but close to it.

Christmas is the season for a blizzard of stuff. It can lead a kid to think it's her birthday. To calm the storm, you may have to first seek cooperation from friends and relatives. Diplomatically explain your thoughts toward overboard gift-giving. Otherwise, they could think you've slipped over the religious edge, wanting to drag them down with you. Ask grandma and grandpa to deliver their gifts this year in a car rather than in last year's Toys-R-Us semi-tractor-trailer.

Make room in your Christmas season for a visit to a children's hospital. Noelle and Rudolph can distribute a share of their sleigh of presents with kids who spend Christmas with no one but the staff. Together, you and the kids sort through their toys — not just the broken, pieces-missing, back-of-the-closet rejects, but some good ones that have streamed in at Christmas and over the past year. Likely, the hospital staff will be so impressed that they'll offer your kids a little gift. That's nice of them, but it sort of defeats the purpose. Ask, instead, that it be included with your kids' donations.

Will Noelle and Rudolph be eager to contribute? "Remember, Mom, we have to leave first thing tomorrow morning to give away our stuff." Did you ever have to instruct them as toddlers, "Now, remember, kids, keep all your toys to yourself. Don't share!" It does not come naturally to kids, or adults either, to part freely with what is *"Mine!"* But it is very good and liberating to do so.

A consuming pursuit of worldly riches is more than a misguided distraction. It's an unsatisfying dead-end. It puts the focus on that which fades, "where moth and rust consume" (Matthew 6:19). The more time and energy spent toward accumulation, the less time spent toward God and others.

No wonder Jesus so vehemently warned, "Where your treasure is, there will your heart be also." He knew well all the snares present in clutching finite treasure over infinite treasure.

14

Stop It

Therefore do not be anxious about tomorrow,
for tomorrow will be anxious for itself. Let the
day's own trouble be sufficient for the day.

—Matthew 6:34

The comedian Bob Newhart is known for his impish vignettes poking fun at human foibles. In one, he plays a psychologist who claims to have perfected a revolutionary technique guaranteed to obliterate emotional distress in under five minutes—at a cost of only five dollars, no less. Though he assures, "Most people don't need to spend the whole five dollars."

Eager to be quickly "cured," a young woman settles in and begins her tale of fear. While admitting that nothing of the sort is ever likely to happen, she remains controlled by its mind-tormenting presence. After less than a minute of rapt listening, the good doctor introduces his technique—a sharply voiced: "Stop it!" Momentarily flustered, the young patient begins again. Once more, Newhart commands, this time louder: "Stop it!" After each of her fretful details, he reiterates another firm: "Stop it!" Finally, she questions how his supposed fix is of any benefit to her. He responds, "Do you like being this way?" Not at all. "Then stop it!"

That's it? "Stop it?" Surely, that's not even worth the five bucks. To stop it, one must know *how* to stop it. How to fret less. How to stay calm.

Many, if not most, answers to life's troubles, it is assumed, hinge upon finding the *how*. How do I show my spouse more affection? How can I quit talking about myself so much? How do I eat less and exercise more? How do I pay more attention at church?

Tell me the strategies, the methods, the formulas. What steps do I take to move from point A (losing my temper) to point B (holding my temper)?

My first book was promoted by the publisher as a "how-to" childrearing guide. That was ironic, since the book took aim at the how-to notions corroding parents' confidence and authority. So ingrained is the how-to mindset that even an anti-how-to book was promoted as a how-to. I suppose it could be called a how-to manual for countering how-to manuals.

Are there better ways to parent? To be more affectionate? To listen longer? To lose weight? Sure. But a preoccupation with finding the *how* overlooks what makes any *how* successful: the will, the inner drive to make it succeed.

"Do not be anxious about tomorrow" addresses the will. It directs us to plunge deeper into our yet-to-be-fully-tapped reservoir of resolve. Jesus counsels that the first step toward worrying less is to decide to worry less. Or as Dr. Newhart would put it, to "Stop it!"

One research tool is the meta-analysis. Brainy-sounding name aside, it's a review of a related group of studies, coming to one overall conclusion. In a meta-analysis of weight-loss plans, the reviewers singled out the "will to lose" as critical to success. A program's particulars mattered less than a person's determination to shed pounds. Those who did well focused their full will toward doing well.

Stop It

"Do you want to be here?" — a question I ask clients upon first coming to me. Shouldn't the answer be obvious? After all, the individual scheduled the visit. The question really asks, "Are you willing to do what it takes to improve your marriage? Your family? Your mood? Your anxiety level?"

Giving someone good ideas is part of counseling. Motivating someone to transfer those ideas from the office to life is the hard part.

My brother and I have lifted weights together for nearly forty years. In my twenties, I felt like I was lifting on the moon. Now, I feel like I'm lifting on Jupiter. (Remember your physics?) A beginner might ask us, "How do you keep coming in? What's the secret for staying with this?" Our answer: "There are no secrets. Just show up." Some days, exercise invigorates. Some days, it drains. No matter, just keep showing up. Don't internally debate whether or not today is a go-day or a skip-day. Be an automaton. Grab your stuff, climb into the car, and walk through the gym door. Gains will follow.

"Do not be anxious about tomorrow." Could yesterday be substituted for tomorrow? As a group, psychologists don't read much of Jesus' life book, but they do take pages from it, however unknowingly. They talk much about "living for today" or "living in 'the now.'" Reaching back to undo the past is an impossible stretch. You can blunt the past's reverberations, apologize for them, and learn from them, but even so, all undoing has to happen in the present. To be anxious about the past is to chain oneself to what is passed. Jesus implies that anxiety must not travel into yesterday. God's grace moves not backward but forward, turning old wrongs into long gones.

"For tomorrow will be anxious for itself." Anxiety commands the top of the emotional distress scale. Its only rival is depression. Anxiety presents several sides. The first side is a general uneasiness across social situations. The second is one or more irrational fears that can be near paralyzing. Its third side is its most fearsome—the "panic attack," a sudden, inexplicable physical eruption.

President Franklin Roosevelt, on the abyss of World War II, reassured the country with the memorable line, "The only thing we have to fear is fear itself." These words would apply to lessening anxiety. Be less anxious about being anxious, and anxiety will lose intensity.

Some years ago, I was at softball practice. At the time, I could order my legs, "Run," and they dutifully obeyed. For over an hour, I shagged fly balls hit to me. Shortly after running down one well-hit ball, my heart started banging in my chest, my breathing came in gasps, and I felt light-headed. Well, what did I expect? I had just sprinted. Rather than easing, though, the adrenaline surge built. I left the field to sit and calm myself.

So, this is what a panic attack feels like, I thought. Many clients have told me about similar experiences, which had prompted not a few to head for the nearest emergency room. As it happened, I didn't add head panic to body panic. Instead, I became a detached observer of the whole episode, anxious (forgive the pun) to analyze it.

Because panic attacks are typically not spurred by underlying health dangers, I was reasonably sure I had little cause for worry. Consequently, my anxiety level did not escalate into a physiological feedback loop in which it fed upon itself. For reasons unknown to me, my body had kicked off a "fight or flight" reaction. Within fifteen minutes, all my systems settled to near-normal. Though I'll admit, I did have some leftover angst at dropping that last fly ball.

At a post-practice meal, I realized that distracted by a busy day, I hadn't eaten in over twenty-four hours. My blood sugar had likely plummeted. That final sprint initiated a physical cascade resulting in a panic attack.

Nothing comparable has happened since. Well, that's not completely true. I did feel pangs of panic when my teenage son once handed me his report card along with a list of successful entrepreneurs who had never graduated high school.

Had I overanalyzed that curious ball practice incident (What? A psychologist, overanalyzing?), I risked anticipatory anxiety, a nagging worry that more of the same is coming. When and where? During a game? In the last inning? With me at bat? And the score tied? The fear of anxiety reemerging makes it more likely to reemerge. Anxiety begets anxiety.

What-ifs are major instigators of anxiety. A what-if is an ongoing fretfulness about some future adversity, whether it's likely to happen or not. What if I get seriously ill? What if I lose my job? What if my children act immorally? What if they leave the Faith?

What-ifs are limited only by one's imagination. Though what-ifs can arrive, our Lord exhorts: Don't allow them to occupy your mind. Today will be robbed of peace, and tomorrow will ruin your today.

A peace-robbing what-if for expectant parents is, "What if my baby is not born healthy?" Happily, most babies arrive well and thriving. Even when not, though, moms and dads are often surprised that they not only adapt better than they feared, but their former fear has turned to blessing. Once again, to cite Psychological Truth #105: We don't always predict accurately how we will react to future events.

The movie *Jaws*[12] splashed a hellish star onto the screen, a seemingly demonic great white shark set on terrorizing a quiet New England resort town. As *Jaws* gathered viewers, actual beaches lost visitors.

"What if a shark attacks me while I'm in the ocean?" That angst sunk its teeth into psyches everywhere. Shark attacks, in fact, are extremely rare. Yet new what-ifs waved in due to a far-fetched

---

[12] Directed by Steven Spielberg, performances by Roy Scheider and Richard Dreyfuss, Universal Pictures, 1975.

fictional flick. Just shows how easily what-ifs can constrict our freedom.

Don't bring tomorrow's troubles into today, says the Lord. Today has enough trouble of its own. Let tomorrow's troubles come tomorrow, if they do at all. *What if* you tried thinking this way? And if you're still fretting about tomorrow, just "stop it!"

15

Am I Good or What?

*Thus when you give alms, sound no trumpet
before you. . . . Do not let your left hand
know what your right hand is doing.*

—Matthew 6:2–3

Quit the showboating. Cut the performance. Close the show.

All say the same thing: "Who are you trying to impress?"
Grandstanding for the crowd doesn't thrill the crowd. It sends
them searching for the nearest exit. Showing off is cute, circa age
two or so. Much past that, it courts the reverse reaction sought.

Someone's talents or abilities, however shiny, dim when linked
with, "Are you paying attention? Is the camera on me?" The
luster dulls even faster with a waft of, "Don't you wish you could
be like me?"

Jesus preached to a society steeped in religious regulations.
The keepers of the regulations thought themselves the elect. They
were the celebrities—our rock stars, athletes, and video VIPs.
They knew Jewish law and were quick to let everyone know how

well. Their elevated status sired pride, a superior "you're not the righteous person I am."

Jesus sternly instructed both them and us, "Beware of practicing your piety before men in order to be seen by them.... And when you pray, you must not be like the hypocrites; for they love to stand and pray in the synagogues and at the street corners, that they may be seen.... When you pray, go into your room and shut the door" (Matthew 6:1-6).

His warning: Don't let religion deform into religiosity, holiness to pious performance, and pleasing God to pleasing people.

Ours is far-removed from the God-centered atmosphere of first-century Palestine. Now just as then, however, faith-guided people gravitate toward like-minded others, seeking connection and support within their circle. Thus, the temptation lurks to measure ourselves against those around us. How well am I doing? Who better serves the Church? Who is more prayerful? Who is raising lots of children? Who can pray the Rosary in Aramaic while kneeling on broken glass, except when levitating?

Thinking myself above you because my house is bigger and fancier, with a backyard gazebo no less, or because my son just won his third Student of the Month Award, while yours just got his first A, is wrong enough. Even more wrong is thinking myself above you because I believe God agrees with me.

For some years, I separated myself from the Catholic Church. I wasn't angry with Her. My thinking was sloppy: God is God, Jesus is Jesus—what's it matter where I worship? I was a culturally fashionable atheist; there is a God, but He thinks a lot like me.

The church I attended offered a Sunday Bible study. One question was, "Why do people get so irked by us Christians, particularly by our moral beliefs?" One answer: Those beliefs convict them. Deep down is a God-light still flickering, and we're reminding them of that.

Am I Good or What?

But another question nagged at me. Is it my "virtue" that both-
ers others, or is it something less virtuous? Do I live what I profess,
or do I make sure they know I do? Do I come across as holy or as
"holier-than-thou?" Am I being likeable or a jerk? If I wished to
push someone away from me, or much worse away from God, I'd
be hard-pressed to find a better—or worse—demeanor.

Jesus said, "When you give alms, sound no trumpet before you."
This referred to parading through the streets, heralded by a horn
which blared, "Take notice! A person of importance is coming
through."

We have moved far beyond using a single horn to announce
our presence. We now have a whole orchestra. Its name is social
media. It enables us to parade through countless streets. No longer
do others have to leave their houses to watch us; we can enter theirs.

Snapface, Instaflick, Spacebook—I can't keep up with all the
names—are not without their good sides. They are cyber-paths
for family and friends to travel together. Not all self-news is self-
publicity, of course. The difference is that self-news lacks ego. It
says, "I'm pleased to share this with you," rather than, "Take notice.
I'm worth knowing all about."

Because of its limitless reach, social media is a supremely seductive venue for limitless self-promotion ("selfies") to make me
look special. "The video of my son, Pele, scoring the winning
soccer goal yesterday had one hundred twenty-six views, forty-
seven likes, and twenty-one shares. And I didn't even post that
he's the only six-year-old playing in a league for seven-year-olds.
I'll do that tonight."

Then, too, social media applause isn't always real applause.
It may merely reflect high-tech etiquette, a ritual response to a
ritual stimulus. A fair number of those on the receiving end think,
"What's so special about her bagel with an inch of peanut butter
for breakfast?" Have you harbored like thoughts during a catalogue

of "look at what I'm doing today" posts? Did you return a thumbs-up anyway?

Most everyone who gives and receives Christmas cards finds a handful of family updates tucked inside, chronicles of the past year's doings. Some are unpretentious: "Greetings from the Noelles." Others are not-so-thinly disguised brag epistles. Admit it, you don't read the full book-length script until Groundhog Day, if then.

"My daughter, Bliss, turned eleven and just completed her tenth year of ballet, gymnastics, competitive powerlifting, and Greco-Roman language scholarship. She's been busy gearing up for her Olympic tryouts in 2024. We're hoping she'll be able to multitask that with her pending nomination as Junior Ambassador to NATO.

"Her brother Noble was surprised on his sixth birthday with calls from the pope, the president, and two of the former Beatles. His party had to be cut short because we all had to leave for a week-long cruise honoring him for winning our state's 2020 First Grader of the Year Award.

"My husband, Forbes, has been named regional sales manager for the Northeast section of the Milky Way, while I keep active volunteering at the nursing home ten to twelve hours a day, knitting shawls for the residents and teaching them sign language.

"The real go-getter of the family, though, is big brother, Sterling, who just last week…"[13]

Social media can be a daily Christmas letter on steroids. The rewards (techno-stickers?) that keep social media zooming along are the reached-for numbers of virtual kudos — "likes" and thumbs-ups.

Social media relates using pictures. Face to face, people relate using words. We are more verbal than visual. Thus, if one is self-focused, words are his main currency. Someone somewhere once

[13] Excerpt from *Raising Upright Kids in an Upside Down World*, by Dr. Ray Guarendi, EWTN Publishing, 2020, 60.

said, "Don't tell others who you are. Let them find out for themselves. They'll remember it longer."

Survey one hundred people. "How many minutes can you listen to someone drone on and on about himself, his family, his success, his wealth, and his humility before you tune out?" Survey says three. "How many excuses do you concoct to leave the conversation?" Survey says four. "How many brag-brimming monologues have you endured before automatically walking out of the room as soon as he walks in?" Survey says six.

While not the top conversation crusher (nastiness and disrespect claim that spot), bragging is a close second. It sabotages give-and-take conversations. It also sabotages give-and-take relationships.

What is it about long-winded boasting that is so grating? It's what's spoken: I'm something. And what's unspoken: You're not.

So? What does it matter what someone thinks about himself or about me? Why can't I just listen until the wind subsides? Because lopsided conversations aren't enjoyable. They strain patience. Besides, I, too, may want to talk a little. Some conversation competition tugs at most of us.

Brag talk has two strains—acute and chronic. Acute is the more usual. It's a limited intrusion into a conversation and typically not the overall topic. Chronic brag talk is far more abrasive. It dominates an exchange, if you can call it that.

Whether acute or chronic, stifle brag talk, says Jesus. We are to regard ourselves as "lowly servants." St. Paul repeats Jesus, "Count others better than yourselves" (Philippians 2:3), a gauntlet thrown down to today's trendy self-esteem gospel. It's straightforward: The more I'm interested in me, the less I'm interested in you.

Have you ever met someone, chatted a while, and walked away with an altogether favorable first impression? What made her so likeable? Then you realized: She was genuinely absorbed in you. She asked about your family, your career, your interests, your faith.

Jesus, The Master Psychologist

She effortlessly kept the conversation on you, not being nosey, but pleasant. A little unsettling, isn't it, to see how easily we let it happen?

My teenage son once asked me, "Dad, how do I talk to a girl so that she's comfortable with me?" My wife was nearby, wearing a look of, "Let's see if Ray has learned anything since we dated."

"Jon, talk more about her than you." Enter her world, her likes and dislikes, schooling, and career plans. Ask her questions. Let her answers lead to more interest. You'll practically guarantee a smooth first contact.

Preschool teachers are familiar with "parallel play" — two children playing side by side with little or no interest in playing together. Parallel play is a sign of developmental immaturity. It is outgrown with age and better social awareness.

Adults engage in a version of parallel play. Call it "parallel talk." You tell me something about you, then I'll tell you something about me. When I pause, you can talk again. Then, when you pause, the subject returns to me.

You: My daughter just earned a full scholarship — athletic and academic — to Elite University. It was only one of five awarded.

Me: That is great. I remember how excited we were when my son received his scholarship, along with his early admittance letter at age sixteen.

You: My daughter thought about early admittance but was involved in so many activities her senior year that she just wanted to build up her resume. She's not sure what graduate school she'll eventually choose.

Me: That was our situation, too. Our younger son, Lincoln, was president of his "Future Rulers Club," something our family has been involved with for years. I founded the local chapter and was really active at the regional level.

The Lord says: Strive to keep the self subdued. Whether verbal or visual, self-elevation does not draw others closer to us. It pushes them away.

It's to our good that our left hand doesn't always know what our right hand is doing. It's even better that we don't tell others all about what our right hand is doing.

16

The "J" Word

Judge not, and you will not be judged; condemn
not, and you will not be condemned.

—Luke 6:37

An evangelical pastor notes that the Bible verse he'd long heard most often quoted was John 3:16, "For God so loved the world that he gave his only Son, that whoever believes in him should not perish but have eternal life."

John 3:16 has since fallen into second place, he says, behind "do not judge." Left unspoken is "me." The verse is favored by those who otherwise ignore or reject many of Jesus' other teachings. What's more, the verse is routinely loosed upon those who do want to follow Jesus' other teachings. At least they're quoting the Bible, even if cherry-picking it.

The religious powers opposing Jesus judged who was good and who was bad and who was headed where at life's end. Jesus shocked them: "The tax collectors and prostitutes will get into Heaven before you." No doubt furious, they thought, "What?! Those human dregs? Wretched sinners going into Heaven before us, the law-abiding? Now, we are even more sure you're a false prophet."

In so many words, Jesus told them: You are quite wrong. You can't know anyone's soul. That knowledge is my Father's alone.

Is Jesus telling us, "Be slow to judge right from wrong. Stay open-minded about morality"? That can't be. Repeatedly, He charges me to discern good from bad, under one condition: I am to be governed by His code, not by my personally-crafted one. Nor am I to do moral arithmetic, adding up the total of someone's sins which would throw him over salvation's allowable limit. The most sin-sodden individual can repent up to his last breath with no one's awareness but God's.

San Francisco's Golden Gate Bridge is a famous tourist attraction. It's also famous for something darker: suicidal leaps. Once jumping, almost no one survives. One man did, though, later writing about his instantaneous regret and sorrow. To an observer, he sought self-destruction. To God, he sought contrition.

Mindful of the Good Thief who with his last words turned toward Jesus, the Church offers Masses for those who've died by their own hand, aware that even the most violent suicide may offer a micro-moment for repentance; a moment perhaps too fleeting for our measure, but certainly not for God's.

During therapy, someone will talk of a horribly-lived past, admitting his wrongs and all the ways he's hurt himself and others. With each session, more puzzle pieces complete the picture—alcohol-abusing parent(s), shattered families, little love, no moral guidance. While meaning to overcome his past, why he is who he is slowly becomes clear. At that, the most probing therapy can't untangle all the convoluted knots—social, psychological, spiritual. Doing so would call for a mind of infinite intelligence.

I once held a Bible study at a local jail. Many of the guys had an upbringing close to my own—two loving parents, solid discipline, religious guidance, good education. For some of the guys, these were not only lacking but entirely absent. I've heard, "There but for the grace of God go I." Walking into that jail, I saw it.

More than one child has caused me to wonder, "How likely will this child grow into a well-adjusted adult?" Some kids begin life in a drug-soaked womb. Others absorb years of neglect and maltreatment. Still others get little direction from anyone or anyplace. What does all this do to the head? The heart? The soul?

God's compassion toward His children is immeasurably above our own. He alone can fathom the mix of the colliding fragments of their lives and render an infallible judgment.

An abused three-year-old is a victim. Few would argue he's not. Through age seven, assume he's only absorbed more of the same ugliness or worse. The maltreatment gains momentum through ages eleven, fourteen, eighteen. By age twenty, he has changed from a hurting child to a hurtful adult. So, too, has our image of him changed. We no longer see him as a victim but as an offender, no longer innocent but sinful. Little got better for him over the years, while our view of him got worse, though.

Without question, wrongdoing or evil can't be tolerated or excused even when enough "causes" are mustered to explain it. Individuals and society must protect themselves, while doing whatever possible to mitigate or correct the damage. Christians are among the most obligated to do so.

Where is free will in someone's picture? It is still present and able to guide him to his good. Unless constricted by a serious mental disorder, one remains more or less able to choose right over wrong, though his full freedom may fluctuate across time and circumstances.

The Church has a compassionate teaching on the difference between wrong and responsible. Some conduct is always and everywhere wrong. But how much someone is fully responsible for that conduct may be known only to God.

Jesus, The Master Psychologist

TV talk shows endlessly parade base behavior. Why their high ratings? One, they feed voyeurism, that is, the pleasure reaped by peeking into others' chaotic lives. Two, they drive judgmental one-upmanship: "How can those people be so weird? So idiotic? So morally stunted? I may not be the best person, but I'm certainly not *that* bad."

Alcoholics Anonymous (AA) warns new members against an incoming attitude of, "I'm not like these people. Compared to them, I'm doing all right. Of course, then, I also don't need to work so hard to improve myself."

We may wish to grade ourselves on the curve, but God doesn't, which is to our best interests, because Mother Teresa would crash the scale for everybody.

"Don't judge me. Why are you so critical? I don't judge you." — All hurled at those with God-guided principles. All also hurled hardest and fastest by those with self-defined or no religion.

"Why do they accuse me? I don't say anything about how they live. I know better." Yes, but they know how you think. Staying silent is no longer a shield against their allegations. You must accept—celebrate even—their poor choices with both your mind and your mouth.

"How do they know what I think?" They see how you live, so they assume how you think. Your beliefs, in their minds, are a critique of them, a put-down. "Let your light shine before men" (Matthew 5:16), and if you do, your light will inflame some. They can't, or won't, understand how you can try to live a godly life and yet not believe that they, not living likewise, are lost souls.

Must you hide your deepest convictions? Or reveal them only to like-minded people? Otherwise, be safe and remain a moral sphinx? That's not a Christian's prerogative. We are to speak up diplomatically when we judge it wise, keeping in mind that we are speaking up within a culture whose mindset is, "Whatever I want to do is okay by me. Therefore, it should be okay by you. If it's not, brace yourself to be tagged with the 'J' word."

Slow to judge is fast to forgive. My nitpicking father-in-law, my fickle friend, my crusty neighbor all push me to my limits of endurance. If I can accept that they, as do I, have foibles and quirks, I'll regard them less as jerks and more as those with some jerky ways. It's a softer view.

A video features a young man finding a pair of ordinary looking sunglasses. Donning them, he finds they are anything but ordinary. They enable him to peer into the hidden struggles of those around him. The irritable restaurant server who, hours before, was forced to leave her sick child with a friend. The young, densely tattooed, face-pierced bus rider who at age sixteen had to choose the streets over a chaotic home. The erratic driver who had cut in front of him to rush his son to the hospital emergency room.

Most people in our lives don't carry such heavy loads. Nonetheless, most do live with everyday struggles that are beyond our vision.

Standard news footage: TV cameras turn their probing eyes toward the quiet, church-going family man, coach of his kids' little league team, who, one night, ups and torches four neighborhood garages and two storage sheds. Each interviewed neighbor gives a similar personality profile: "He seemed like such a nice guy—always waved when he drove by and I was outside. At our Labor Day barbecue, he brought over some corn and a dozen donuts. I never would have seen anything like this coming."

Television and radio hosts, after reporting on the criminal or self-indulgent behavior of a high-profile personality, add, "I met him a couple of years ago at a dinner. We spent about an hour talking, and he was a really good guy."

Forming favorable first impressions upon limited contact is understandable. Indeed, it just seems the decent way to be. Look for the good. And it may be confirmed in time that this person is as admirable as first perceived.

Of those who move through our lives, however, we know well only a relative few of them. Most others, we know only a few inches deep. We may have had some brief conversations with them, cheered beside them at our kids' games, volunteered together at church or school, but that's the extent of our relationship. Most personal contacts, even those repeated, don't enable much penetration into someone's personality or morals. Therefore, foregoing judgment comes easier when you know little about someone. There's just not much to judge.

On the other hand, as you come to know a person better, with both her good and her not-so-good qualities, being critical has more openings.

Priests hear no end to sinful conduct. One would expect, after listening to thousands of souls bared, their view of people would become tainted, if not despairing. Instead, they confess that their picture of penitents does not plummet but in fact rises. Yes, they do hear human frailty in all its diversity, but they also hear remorse and resolve to live better. It's an ongoing reminder, they will tell you, to remain compassionate.

Again, to emphasize, this is not at all to say we don't judge conduct, although judging motives is much more difficult, as they are complex and less obvious. We are to have a sturdy sense of right and wrong, as guided by God, not us. Still, the more we get to know someone, the more we see things we don't like or approve of, not necessarily because we're finding out more about their "bad" side, but because we're finding out more about them, and as with all of us, negatives walk among their positives.

"We're all sinners"; "I'm sure you've done your share of wrong things"; "You're not perfect, you know" — each a truth of our Faith. Also, each voiced by those who suspect you (with or without evidence) are questioning them. In essence, "Who are you to correct me? When you are perfect, then you can talk." If perfect were the standard, no one could talk to anyone about morality at all.

"I love you—I just don't like what you did." "Your behavior was bad, but you're not bad." "What you did wasn't good, but you're good." So say parents wanting to reassure their kids that misbehavior doesn't personally devalue them. Though well-meant, the reasoning flies over most kids' heads. Little Justice's elementary thinking is, "I acted bad; therefore, I am bad." With maturity, he should come to understand how he can still be loved even when acting unlovable.

Unfortunately, many adults haven't yet matured past, "If you don't accept what I do, then you don't accept me. Further, to accept me, you must applaud me." It's a leap of illogic not yet outgrown.

A folksy little ditty offers a light summary on this whole topic:

> I was shocked, confused, bewildered
> As I entered heaven's door,
> Not by the beauty of it all,
> Nor the lights or the décor.
>
> But it was the folks in heaven
> Who made me sputter and gasp—
> The thieves, the liars, the sinners,
> The alcoholics and the trash.
>
> There stood the kid from seventh grade
> Who swiped my lunch money twice.
> Next to him was my old neighbor
> Who never said anything nice.
>
> Bob, who I always thought
> Was rotting away in hell,
> Was sitting pretty on cloud nine,
> Looking incredibly well.

Jesus, The Master Psychologist

I nudged Jesus, "What's the deal?
I would love to hear your take.
How'd all these sinners get up here?
God must've made a mistake.

And why is everyone so quiet,
So somber — give me a clue."
"Hush, child," He said, "they're all in shock,
No one thought they'd be seeing you."[14]

Jesus' guidance is clear. We are to judge right and wrong by God's standards. We are not to judge someone's standing in the eyes of God. We must also be ready to be misunderstood for our principles, or, in a word, judged.

---

[14] J. Taylor Ludwig, "Folks in Heaven."

17

Give and You'll Get

Let the greatest among you become as the
youngest, and the leader as one who serves.

—Luke 22:26

A group of elderly people were asked about "personal life satisfaction." As expected, a broad social network—family and friends
—leads to happier later years.

Unexpected, however, was that a broad social network gives the
elderly more avenues to serve as volunteers, mentors, confidantes,
or child caretakers, to name a few. Serving not only prolongs youth,
it energizes aging.

I asked a priest, "What, for you, is the strongest piece of evidence
for the truth of Christianity?" Without hesitation, he replied, "The
system works."

What system? Church authority? Worship devotions? Prayers?
Sacraments? He meant the moral system—what Christ gave as
the best way to live. It's a system glaringly at odds with the ever-
evolving secular formulas for fulfillment. Nonetheless, it proves
itself worthy of trust as a sure road to "personal life satisfaction."

Jesus, The Master Psychologist

Altruism is defined as "an unselfish concern for the welfare of others." It is at the heart of Jesus' "system." And researchers are noticing. Studies repeatedly confirm that serving others brings a bevy of personal benefits. To quote St. Paul who is quoting Jesus, "It is more blessed to give than to receive" (Acts 20:35). Most studies probably wouldn't use the word "blessed."

"People who help others may be rewarded with better mental health.... Researchers ... suggest that altruism offers benefits that can help counter the negative effects of stressful life events."[15]

Translation: The more one serves, the better he copes with his troubles.

"Our findings underscore the value of altruistic attitudes ... in fostering life satisfaction and positive effects in old age."[16] If good for the older, then altruism must be good for the younger.

"Evidence shows that helping others is actually beneficial to your mental health and well-being."[17] "Actually?" Is that a revelation? If so, it's two thousand years old.

Altruism has a relative: gratitude. "It's not unusual for people to experience a 'grass is greener' feeling from time to time. However, because good deeds are often done for those who are going through a difficult time, the experience can serve to remind helpers that their own lives are actually pretty good. Sometimes, actually seeing what is on 'the other side of the fence' can make you feel thankful for what you have."[18]

---

[15] "Helping Others Helps Your Own Mind," WebMD, October 21, 2003.

[16] Kahana et al., "Altruism, Helping, and Volunteering: Pathways to Well-Being in Late Life," *Journal of Aging and Health* 25, no. 1 (February 2013).

[17] "Doing Good Does You Good," Mental Health Foundation, 2020.

[18] Sherrie Bourg Carter, "Helper's High: The Benefits (and Risks) of Altruism," *Psychology Today*, September 4, 2014.

Youthful aging, stress reduction, mental and physical well-being, and now gratitude — the positives keep piling up.

It seems counterintuitive. As more of my wants are met, shouldn't I be more satisfied? Society assures me: "Of course!" It also advises me to turn my wants into "needs." Needs are more urgent. They demand being fulfilled more so than wants.

Serving, says our Lord, will meet more of my "needs" than will being served. What's more, as my "needs" list expands, it will outpace my sense of fulfillment. Such explains why so many of those most idolized and indulged have surprisingly high rates of depression, marital breakups, drug and alcohol abuse, and suicide. "Getting" and "grateful" don't always hold hands. Too much getting has a habit of letting go of grateful's hand.

"I've spoiled him. He gets what he wants most of the time. You'd think he'd be okay with the few times he doesn't. Instead, he gets madder." So say parents frustrated by little Conan's demanding behavior.

The more anyone — young or old — gets his way, the less he can tolerate when he doesn't. Getting appeased at ninety percent dramatically drops one's ability to accept the ten percent when he doesn't. The more one is served, the less his desire to serve.

"Satisfy yourself, then you can satisfy others." "You must like yourself before you can like others." "Meet your own needs so you can meet others." Jesus turns these self-esteem mantras on their heads: Serve others first, you will then be satisfied. Like others first, and you will like yourself.

Should someone neglect my "needs," as I see it, my resentment can follow. My well-being is being underserved. "He seldom considers what I want." "What matters to me doesn't matter to her." "Every so often, you'd think they'd think about me."

During counseling, a client might complain, "I'm tired of giving. I give and I give. I'm going to start focusing on me for a change."

Contrary to her claim, she may be someone who for some time has been more concerned about herself. She's not moving from giving to getting. A giving person doesn't count how much she gives. She doesn't keep personal score. Moreover, a good person doesn't bask in how good she is.

Recall the Law of Social Reciprocity: If I treat you well, you should treat me well. If I help you, you should help me. If I serve you, you should serve me.

Jesus charges us: Break that law. Seek to serve. If others reciprocate, be grateful. Don't expect it.

18

A Hard Teaching

Everyone who divorces his wife and marries another
commits adultery, and he who marries a woman
divorced from her husband commits adultery.

—Luke 16:18

A Protestant pastor once told a Catholic priest, "If your church ever changes its teaching on divorce and remarriage, we'll see a lot fewer of your people. It's what makes many of them leave you and come to us."

The pastor's droll observation holds true. The Catholic Church's high view of marriage—straight from Her founder—is widely ignored. Only Her prohibition of artificial contraception meets like rebellion.

Is Jesus being unrealistic? In these I-decide-my-own-morals times, do His precepts flow too rapidly against the cultural current? Does He allow for no exceptions? Under no circumstances?

In fact, He does. Using a word that scholars interpret to mean "invalid," Jesus allows that what looks to be a marriage may not be one in reality. Thus, He gives a reason for what is informally called an "annulment"—the finding that a full, genuine commitment from one or both partners was absent from the day of the ceremony.

Jesus decisively closed a gaping marriage loophole of His time. On little more than a whim, a husband could renounce his wife, leaving her destitute and floundering to survive. It was a cruelly callous but widely accepted practice. Jesus sharply commanded, "No more of that!"—words ringing relevant to our own century.

History is a repeating cycle. Our marriage ties are not so unlike the slip knots of two thousand years ago in Palestine. A divorced spouse these days may not be flung into raw survival mode, but may still face plenty of social and emotional reverberations.

No question, some marriages are severely disturbed, ravaged by all sorts of pathologies—alcoholism, abuse, adultery, assaults. The Church knows well that separation may sometimes provide the only protection for a spouse or the children or both. More commonly, though, extreme turmoil isn't present. What is present is one or both spouses feeling too unhappy in the marriage to try to fix it or even endure it. Divorce becomes the preferred option, an intruder standing at the door, knocking steadily.

"If your spouse were to change those things you most dislike about him, would it make any difference to you?" It's a question I ask to those in counseling. A few answer with an outright, "No." Others hesitate, with their silence speaking loudly. Their marriage's "once upon a time" love and goodwill has been waning for so long as to feel irretrievable. As one husband in a movie captured his animus for his wife, "I can't stand the way she licks postage stamps."[19]

"I don't want a divorce, but I see no other choice. Nothing will change." It can certainly look that way, especially if for some time the only change has been downward. At that, even if neither spouse

[19] *Ruthless People*, 1986.

acts to improve anything, circumstances themselves can change, propelling the marriage to a better place. Kids who caused clashes may leave the nest. Money strains ease. Job demands decline. Difficult relatives move from three miles away to three states away. Marriage, as life, is fluid. Little stays static.

Suicide has been called a permanent solution to a temporary circumstance. Meaning, it is an act of irreversible finality. The pain seems intractable, so the only way to lessen it is to leave. Divorce is a form of marital suicide, though not always irreversible. It is expected to solve what appears unsolvable. It is driven by the conviction that little will get better.

A survey asked those who were five years post-divorce, "Are you more content now than you were when married?" Half admitted to presently being as much or more discontent. Of those once seriously contemplating divorce but not acting for whatever reason — religion, kids, finances, fears — five years later, four-fifths reported better marriages. Who would have predicted that? I've spoken to those who years earlier were sure they'd find more fulfillment somewhere else or with someone else. Many now look back at their decision with regrets.

"I've tried to change. It makes no difference." Upon hearing this, I can't know how much effort to change has been made over how long. I do know that we naturally see ourselves less in need of reform than those around us. Never do I hear, "I want marriage counseling, because I've finally realized how difficult I am to live with. And I begged my spouse to join me to help me take a good, hard look at myself." Right. Typically, each wants the other to be fixed. Once again, the Golden Rule is the best fixer: To change another, begin first to change yourself.

A priest friend observed, "Giving up on a marriage often means giving up on the Holy Spirit's healing power." Even should one spouse ignore the Holy Spirit or any part of religion, the other can still pray for persevering grace—if not to soften her spouse's heart, then to soften her own.

"God wants me to be happy." Happiness, counsels the culture, is the ultimate quest. Countless TV characters spout the line, "I just want to be happy" or "All I want for my children is to be happy." Happiness is a peak entitlement, regardless of who or what has to be jettisoned to achieve it. If marriage hinders one's happiness, it can and should be dumped.

God does indeed want happiness for us, but through His way, not ours. Our limited foresight all too often misleads us, away from happiness and toward unanticipated unhappiness.

Is Jesus downplaying all that can unravel a marriage? After all, He never married, so He never endured the stress of a struggling marriage. If He were only human, Jesus couldn't speak from personal experience. He is, however, the God-man. He has full awareness of the pain that can penetrate a union. Why, then, is He so adamant about commitment?

"People divorce too easily these days, but in my case, I think I have good reason." Jesus knows that easing open the divorce door would incite a crowded rush through it. And it has. The statistics confirm it: Forty-plus percent of first-time marriages fail. Second unions, often meant to escape the deficiencies of the first, fail at even greater rates. Sixty years ago, divorce interrupted about ten percent of all marriages. Human nature doesn't change. So, how did most of those in past generations stay together "till death do us part?" If it is unrealistic today, why wasn't it unrealistic then?

"It's not good for anybody to stay together just for the kids." It's the grown-ups, more so the expert types, who proclaim this, and not the kids. They are confident: Bad marriages are bad for kids. Big people trouble trickles downward. Supposedly, the children would be better off, or at least less worse off, moving back and forth between parents. The distance will cushion conflicts for everybody.

A Hard Teaching

It's a nice theory, plausible-sounding on paper. Real life shreds it. Plenty of parents find that separate households don't lead to a truce or a more peaceful coexistence. They might ease the former day-to-day strife, but they introduce new trials.

Social science renders few verdicts with more evidence than "bad marriages are bad for kids." No, wait, I have that wrong. The evidence actually says, "Divorce is bad for children." Hundreds of studies obliterate the claim that "the kids will be fine," an empty claim often used to comfort the exiting spouse.

Yes, some kids will be fine, due to innate resilience or because both parents are cooperating to smooth the kids' new lives. As the little ones who ally with mom and dad equally become more independent-minded teenagers, however, their relationship with the one who "broke up our family" can slip. More than a few parents have come to me desperately seeking how to reconnect with a child who no longer wants anything to do with them.

What if we were to ask the kids? "Do you want your parents to separate? Would you rather live in one home with two grown-ups who right now aren't getting along, or in two different homes?" After forty years of talking with children, big and little, I know how most would answer.

"Why are they staying together? Why don't they just split and get it over with?" So ask some children. Their question quite often stems from exasperation. They're witnessing a bunch of childish behavior from those supposed to be grown-ups. Divorce is not what the kids want; it's what they're bracing themselves to accept.

"We've agreed to stay together until the kids are raised." Such isn't always a mutual accord. Sometimes, one spouse is itching to go but for now is compromising. Once more, the research is clear: Divorce isn't only bad for the kids at home, it's bad for those who've left the nest. Most young adults wish their family had never fractured. They continue to face divided loyalties, struggles relating to who's now living with whom, coming to suspect the whole idea of marriage. After so many years, their parents still ended up going their separate ways. What does that say about the durability of marital unions?

"I love my kids. I would never do anything to hurt them." So professes nearly every parent walking out on a marriage. No doubt, they do love their kids. The question is: What to them is "love?" Is it love second to self-love? Is it a love that says, "I would never do anything to hurt my children; therefore, what I'm about to do won't hurt them?"

For some time, they likely have felt more warmth for their kids than for their spouse. What better incentive to work longer and harder "for the sake of the kids?" Love for the children can be the catalyst to bring love back into the marriage.

Questions many of those on the edge of divorce don't foresee: How much of your influence will you lose because of split custody or limited visitation? How much of your supervision? Who might enter their mother or father's life as a new romance, and thus enter theirs? Will there be stepchildren? What will they be like? Undisciplined? Nasty? Abusive? Will your children take a backseat to the new spouse's children or to any children conceived in the new relationship? What about finances? Will you have to work longer and harder to make ends meet, leaving less time for moments of togetherness? How much will formerly good family ties, both yours and hers, fray or unravel? Most urgently, are you sure you've worked at this marriage as long and as hard as you are capable?

"I've always said that if my spouse ever cheated on me, the marriage would be over. I couldn't live with someone I couldn't trust." To their surprise, not a few betrayed spouses face Psychological Truth #105: We don't always react as we predicted, especially when facing a highly-charged crisis.

Their former rock-solid resolve never to brook infidelity begins to crack, more so if the wandering spouse is genuinely repentant and seeking to reconcile. Their conviction that the union would be dissolved is now open to rethinking, as they find themselves wanting healing and reunion.

It must be said again: Many spouses are abandoned against their will. They are most willing to give their all to save their marriage. Their spouse isn't. To couples in marriage counseling, I might ask, "Do you want to be here?" Sometimes, a spouse will silently stare at me. It's soon apparent that he or she is just going through some therapeutic motions to allege, "I tried therapy, it didn't work." It is their final proof that the marriage was unsalvageable.

There are those few who commit to their marriage bond post-legal divorce. They believe Christ: A valid marriage is unbreakable, no matter what civil law declares. Because they will not seek another relationship, they are not so much admired and respected but are more critiqued or seen as foolish.

"Move on. It's time. Find someone else. She's not coming back." They know that. They aren't naïvely clinging to a frayed marital thread. They mean to follow their Faith. For that, they are cultural aliens, who are experiencing Christ's warning, "They persecuted me; they'll persecute you."

Jesus' words on marriage and divorce are bold and definite. They are aimed directly at our dominant marital attitudes. As such, the majority, including many Christians, reject them. Modern commitments are supposed to come with room to maneuver.

Jesus leaves little justification for abandoning one's family. More than anyone, Jesus knows how much is at stake, not only for the family, but for all of society.

19

Small Words; Big Effect

And do not swear by your head,
for you cannot make one hair white or black.
Let what you say be simply "Yes" or "No."

—Matthew 5:36–37

Were Jesus walking among us today, He would no doubt note that a person's hair color might pass through multiple variations per year, sometimes per month, sometimes in colors not found in nature. Two thousand years ago, hair hue changed only with one's age. What color God gave, one lived with. Jesus also gave uncolored words: Be concise and mean it.

Buttressing one's words by calling in backup was a practice Jesus heard all around Him. People swore by the gods, by their ancestors, by Heaven, by earth, by just about anyone or anything they could co-opt to cosign their pledge. Doing so, they reckoned, would guarantee their integrity, or at the least assuage their hearer's skepticism.

Jesus said no to this empty practice: Make your yes or your no all that is said. If your yes or no by itself is suspect, what is gained by citing a witness, one who has no say in being cited, and who becomes a collaborator in your declaration, be it true or false?

To quasi-quote Rod Serling, host of the iconic TV show the *Twilight Zone*,[20] "Imagine, if you will, a world where everyone's word is perfectly reliable, where one's word is one's bond." On this side of the twilight zone, no such world exists. Jesus tells His followers to make it exist on their side of the world.

Like the ancients, we moderns practice our own brand of witness collaboration. Though we don't call upon the dead or the inanimate, we do call upon the living. "I'm not the only one who thinks you act that way. Your mother thinks so, too." "You may not want to agree with me about this, but I could name five people who do." "Almost everybody I've talked to sees this my way and not yours."

Citing witnesses is a dirty communication trick. It is a tactic exploited to prove just how wrong you are because you disagree with me. After all, you need to know that I have votes on my side. Of course, the possibility exists that I'm shaping their words to fit my agenda. Then, too, my witnesses might be shocked or distressed if they find that I named them in my case against you.

Jesus abhors witness tampering. We are to be our own witness. True words speak for themselves. They don't need others to speak for them.

Relationships fray when one's yes or no is murky, when yes can mean "maybe" or "for now" or "whatever" or "depending on my mood," and likewise when no means "maybe" or "for now" or "whatever" or "we'll see" (a parent's go-to answer).

Jesus' straightforward words guide parents well. Waxing way beyond yes or no can quickly morph into word windiness—scolding, re-reminding, interminable lecturing. Giving Liberty a yes seldom needs any more explanation, as it agreeably grants him what

[20] CBS Television, 1959–1964.

he wants. In his mind, enough said. A no is the answer that can provoke exhausting overtalking. After forty minutes of debating Liberty, how likely is he to reward you with, "Now I get it, Mom. You're not bucking for Tyrant Parent of the Decade Award. You want what's best for me. Had you stopped twenty minutes back, I wasn't ready to see it your way. Thank you for going the extra twenty." The difference between a twenty-minute monologue and a forty-minute one is that forty is twice as likely to end ugly.

Suppose your first and, in your judgment, final answer to a child's absolutely must-have perk, privilege, or permission is no. Soon, however, you begin to wobble, not because you rationally rethink things, but because you are beleaguered and badgered. Kids rival trial lawyers at squeezing a no into a yes or a "we'll see."

A scenario:

Mario: Look, Mom. Mom, look. Here's that video game I was telling you about! The one I keep seeing on TV. It's really neat, and you said I could get it.

Mom: No, I never said you could get it. I said, "We'll see."

In parent talk, "we'll see" doesn't mean yes or no. It means no decision. In kid talk, "we'll see" means yes is on the horizon, prompted if need be by some well-targeted nagging.

Unless Mom really does mean yes, it's smart to ditch the "we'll see." It is asking for a protracted verbal tug-of-war.

Mom: You've got plenty of video games. Grandma just bought you two more for your birthday. Besides, I don't know anything about this game.

Mario: Yes, you do. I told you before. It's the one where you have to drive a car through all kinds of other cars and see how fast you can get someplace. It's really cool!

Mom: It doesn't sound "really cool" to me. It sounds reckless. Anyway, forget it for this time around.

"This time around?" Is that a "forget it?" Is that a no? Is it another "we'll see?" Is Mom unwittingly asking for more of the same next time around? And the next? In an effort to end the exchange for now, she's leaving it open for down the road.

Mario: Those ones that Grandma got me are for little kids. All they do is show you how to do some math stuff that I already know.

Mom: Good. It won't hurt you to practice. You don't know your math facts all that well.

Mario: Aw, come on, Mom. Just this one game. Then I won't ask for any more for a long time. Promise!

The next step after an appeal to a parent's "reason" has failed is an appeal to emotions. If that lands on a stony heart, execute the fatigue factor. Wear the big person down.

Mario: Mom, I already played it once at Chevy's house. His dad even played it with us. Please, Mom. It's my favorite of all the games. Please, huh?

Mom: No, Mario. Now, that's it. I'm not going to argue about this anymore.

Mario: Mom, look. See it says, "For ages eight and up." I'm ten. It's even got three stars on it, because *School Mountain* says it's a good game for coordination.

Mom may be ready to quit arguing, but Mario isn't. He's keeping his foot on the accelerator. She'll have to be the one to slam on the brakes.

Mom: You can keep nagging all you want, Mario. It's not going to work. I am not buying *Car Maniac* for you.

Mom is noticing the looks on the faces of nearby shoppers, especially those with no children in tow. Giving a teen forty dollars per hour plus benefits to babysit while she shops alone doesn't sound so outrageous now.

Mario: If I can't have it this time, maybe next time? When we get home, I'll show you what games we can get rid of because I don't play them anymore. We can give them to kids who don't have any. I'll give away five for this one, okay?

Mom: We'll see.[21]

Between adults, a yes comes easy. Sometimes, too easy. It sounds full of social grace, though it's empty of follow-through. "For sure, Grandma, I'll be back to see you again real soon." *Real soon* then stretches into six months and counting.

"Oh, yeah, just give me a call, and I'll head over to help you out with that." Three calls later, appreciate that caller ID.

"Good to see you! It's been too long. Let's get together for lunch. I'll text you."

In each situation, I leave feeling good about myself. For the moment, I sounded agreeable. But a yes or its equivalent that doesn't fulfill its promise is only faux-agreeable. It is social fluff. In the end, the yes is a no.

Brevity has a bonus. Most people like hearing it. They've too often been drenched in a downpour of words when a drizzle could have said as much. They might even ask, "Is that all?" To which you could answer, "Yep."

---

[21] Excerpt from *Winning the Discipline Debates*, by Dr. Ray Guarendi, Servant Books, 2013.

Our culture multiplies words to sway and impress. Jesus is telling us to quit the multiplying. And you can count on His Word. He wrote the Book on communication.

Is all this clear? Yes or no?

20

A Cheeky Response

*But if anyone strikes you on the right
cheek, turn to him the other also.*

—Matthew 5:39

Is Jesus a pacifist? Does He want His followers to be pacifists? Is He
denying us any right to self-defense or to protect others?

If half of my face is struck, assuming I'm still standing, do I shake
it off? "That didn't hurt. Hit this side." Then after each cheek is
cuffed, does a second right-left cycle begin?

A few Christian groups take Jesus literally. Physical force, they
believe, is not to be in their repertoire. Theirs is not, however,
the traditional understanding, which not only recognizes that a
Christian has a license but sometimes the duty to defend himself
and others from gratuitous harm.

If Jesus means, "No violence whatever, whenever," He ignored
His own injunction when He wielded a whip against the charlatan
moneychangers in the temple. How, then, do we reconcile His
words with His conduct?

Jesus, The Master Psychologist

One, in launching a premeditated assault, tipping merchant tables and scattering their property along with them, Jesus would have sinned.

A Christian absolute is that Jesus is God. Therefore, He must be morally perfect from His earthly Conception to His Ascension into Heaven. Calling His actions in the temple sinful would be neither legitimate nor logical.

Two, Jesus was validating that, under certain circumstances, reacting strongly in the cause of right is allowed, necessary even.

"Turn the other cheek" is shorthand for: Don't reflexively meet aggression with aggression or violence with violence. Resist the impulse to retaliate. If possible, give a brewing situation time to simmer, then cool.

Escalation—each side ratcheting up retaliation—can rapidly send the scene spiraling out of control. Should only one side cease the cycle of an eye for an eye or, if you will, a cheek for a cheek, both sides can save face, literally and symbolically.

No doubt, occasionally a threat must be decisively answered. Fortunately for most of us, these occasions are scarce. Much more every day are verbal assault—insults, affronts, criticism. These prompt nearly all our occasions to TTOC. We psychologists like to speak in abbreviations.

To Palestinian men, a slap on the face delivered deep disrespect. It smacked of, "You're worthless!" Jesus defaced this gesture: Offenses, even those directed to humiliate maximally, won't have power unless you hand it to them. Instead, respond: That didn't hurt as you intended.

Lawyers know that anyone can sue anyone for any reason. That doesn't prove the case has any merit. Likewise, anyone can say anything to you or about you at any time. That doesn't prove their words have any merit. Most insults lack good intent. As such, they don't deserve much credence. Uplifting advice isn't wrapped inside a put-down.

"Turn the other cheek" is a foreign language to anyone ever-more sensitive to ever-less respect. "How can she say that about me?" "Does he think I deserved that?" "She'd better brace herself to receive in the same way she gives."

Boxers train to "slip a punch." That is, they move their head parallel to an incoming blow. It blunts the impact. To incur less emotional bruising, slip the punch of staggering words. Slipping a punch is the pugilistic counterpart to turning a cheek.

Psychology is turning its face toward Jesus' counsel. One study concluded that ignoring slights is emotionally more settling than feeling compelled to correct the slight slinger. As one shrugs off offenses, they lose their sting. It takes more of a verbal punch to be annoyed or feel belittled. In short, no response is a good response.

A slew of my sins—retaliation, gossip, ill will—flare up after another has accosted me unfairly, as I hear it, anyway. I have reason to react, do I not? I'm just evening the score. If they quit, so will I.

Jesus counters such thinking: "My followers are called to higher principles." My cheek-turning doesn't hinge upon whether or not someone turns his, too. I am not justified in doing unto another as he has done unto me. However much others say that I am justified, Christ says that I am not.

Turning a cheek is easier read than done. Self-control is pushed to its limit. The benefits, however, are well worth it.

First, TTOC avoids remorse. For the moment, a slap for a slap may seem fair. Only later do I regret my words which should have never hit the air.

Second, hard-hitting words resist recall. Even if a follow-up apology softens the blow, they still leave welts. Far better to remain silent than to have to apply emergency first aid to a relationship.

Third, the impulse to swing back surges the instant I am insulted. Turning a cheek buys seconds to cool fevered emotions. Holding my tongue is easier when my face is rotating rather than when my jaw is stiffening.

Were "turn the other cheek" distilled into one word, it would be: "So?" Rather than saying aloud to another, "I can't believe you're accusing me of this!" think to yourself: "So?" Instead of, "I think what you're saying is mean," think: "So?" "You should look at yourself." Again: "So?"

"So?" is a silent word. It stays in your head, not in another's ears. A spoken "So?" is peevish, like a child's comeback to an annoying sibling. A snippy "So?" is not a turned cheek; it's a cheeky retort.

What if someone's slap has merit? Just because it sounds insulting doesn't negate its truth. The flip side of "So?" is "Hmmm." Should I weigh what I'm hearing? Is it an emotional swipe, or does it have substance? Everyone has an untapped reservoir for looking into themselves. We just may be reluctant to do so for fear of what we might see.

Those who occupy small pieces of our lives don't typically push us to our cheek-turning limit. The mail carrier we cross paths with a few times a week—shrugging off her crankiness is time-limited, as within a minute she's gone. As irritating as my daughter's soccer coach can be, the season is only six more games.

It is those who live within our tight social and emotional circle who can test our cheek-turning stamina. Close relations equal more contacts equal more potential for disagreeable words. "My mother has been correcting my discipline since my first child. I'm on child number four." "My brother-in-law talks nonstop about his kids, his job, his house, his golf game. I could tolerate it better if his attitude weren't, 'Yours isn't as good as mine.'"

"Every time I feel one of her jabs, I want to scream." How long has she been jabbing? "For about as long as I've known her." How long is that? "Eighteen years." How many more years of jabbing will convince you that she's not likely to quit? "Why do I have to put up with it?" You might have to, if she's a spouse, parent, in-law, or adult child. Most often, it's better to turn a cheek or to think "So?" than to turn away from a family member.

In my book *Thinking Like Jesus*,[22] I recommend to "close the book." What exactly does that mean? After a number of cheek slaps, end all contact with the slapper? Find reasons to move your face beyond his reach? Leave any room she enters?

"Close the book" means to stop expecting another person to be pleasant, agreeable, fair, or even at least not so difficult. Realize who he is, how he talks, how he acts—yesterday, today, and most likely tomorrow—and you won't be so red-faced around him.

"She needs to know exactly how I feel." "I've about had enough of her remarks." "He needs to be set straight." In other words, "I'm going to clear the air." Most likely, you've already done so more than once. Did you clear the air? Or did you cloud it? Did you hear, "Oh my, I didn't realize I was bothering you that much!" Or did you get a look asking: "What are you talking about?"

If "So?" is one too many words, there is a wordless option: The dumb look. Notice how the face is smack in the middle of so much communication?

Savvy parents know that trying to reason with an unreasonable child regularly hits a dead end. "Why do I need to study? The more I know, the more I forget. And the more I forget, the less I know. So, why study?" Now, I ask you, how can you dispute such logic?

The dumb look is simply a blank stare. It's a smart response upon hearing dumb words. It tacitly says, "Not only won't I react to what I'm hearing, I'm not sure I understand what I'm hearing." Granted, a dumb look comes easier for some of us than others, but anyone with children has had plenty of practice at it.

[22] EWTN Publishing, 2018.

Jesus, The Master Psychologist

Someone once asked me, "What if you just naturally look dumb? How can someone tell if you're giving him a dumb look or just being yourself?" I had no idea how to answer that, so I just gave her a dumb look.

A widespread myth is that if you don't stand up for yourself, you're a doormat. In fact, the truth is quite the opposite. The compulsion to confront can spring from insecurity. "Why would he speak to me like that? Does he think I don't deserve respect?" "She doesn't speak as critically to anybody else. Why just to me?" It takes more self-confidence to turn a cheek than to stiffen a neck.

Turning a cheek, the "So?" and the dumb look — all three can keep you cooler when feeling the heat of unpleasant or unfair words.

A culture that raises assertiveness to a moral virtue is not a culture that rewards turning the other cheek. Rather, it exhorts: Answer word for word any unwarranted or unwanted offense. As with any of Jesus' countercultural commands, however, turning one's cheek proves the best response for both slapper and slappee.

Death? When?

*And I will say to my soul, "Soul, you have
ample goods laid up for many years; take your
ease, eat, drink, be merry." But God said to him,
"Fool! This night your soul is required of you."*

—Luke 12:19–20

"Live like you were dying," the country song counsels.[23] Along with
homespun philosophies, country music also sings of life's hardships.
Hence the joke: What do you get when you play a country song
backward? You get your wife back, your job back, your truck back,
your dog back …

"Live Like You Were Dying" takes a verse from Jesus' music:
Living well here is knowing that living here is transient.

To quote Ben Franklin, "In this world nothing can be said to
be certain, except death and taxes." Death may be certain, but it's
still ignored, even more so than taxes. Though many see death

[23] Single released by Curb Records on June 7, 2004; performed by
artist Tim McGraw; written by Tim Nichols and Craig Wiseman.

come for others, like the party-ready person in Jesus' story, their own end remains ambiguous. The thought of death doesn't interrupt their today.

Jesus is not pushing a morbid preoccupation with death. Such a preoccupation can be a sign of a severe psychological disorder. Furthermore, it can kill the peace Jesus promises in this life. We are to be aware that our days are numbered, but we are not to be emotionally buried by that awareness.

There are no atheists in foxholes. The adage speaks to imminent death reversing a lifetime of apathy toward God. A life-threatening illness can do the same.

Jesus is not addressing those terminally ill or hunkered in the proverbial foxhole. For them, eating, drinking, and being merry is far from their minds. Rather, He is addressing those in seeming good health, warning against filling today with pleasures that will come to little or nothing when their last tomorrow dawns.

The best-selling book *Amusing Ourselves to Death*[24] probes the media and entertainment world's frantic-paced seizing of our senses, all the while dimming our eyes to life's deeper realities. Flashing and beeping titillation absorbs us in "what's next" rather than what matters.

A companion book might be titled *Distracting Ourselves to Death*. Running ever-faster while going nowhere, much like a hamster in a rodent wheel, reaching for more goodies, activities, and recognition gets us no closer to where life is ultimately headed.

Those in the zest and zeal of youth understandably think little about their own passing. To them, today stretches so distant as to seem interminable. Aging, with its nagging reminders of decline, does not intrude into their immediate experience. Only after long decades do they look back, astonished at how fast aging has

[24] Neil Postman, Viking Penguin, 1985.

arrived. "Don't Blink"[25] is another philosophizing country song, which notes the rush of years as viewed through one's rearview mirror.

Our language reflects the belief that life should be long. For example, "middle age" typically refers to the years forty-five to sixty. By extension, "full age" would fall between ninety and one hundred twenty. Despite the twentieth century's meteoric rise in life expectancy, ninety is still only reached by a small group, and one hundred twenty is reached by none.

At his fiftieth birthday, a friend was told, using a golf analogy, "Well, you're now heading into the back nine." He wryly replied, "That would leave me with nine more to play—another fifty years." Making a quick-course correction, he then added, "Right now, I'm probably playing hole eleven or twelve."

"His death was unexpected." No death is completely unexpected when one accepts that death at any time is a possibility, however improbable. Death is only unexpected if it's supposed to be predictable. When not expected, it is seen as a quirk of existence, a thief stealing one's fair share of life. Jesus exhorts us to live as though death can come at its own time, and not ours.

In the miniseries *Jesus of Nazareth*,[26] the rebel crucified next to Christ rebukes the other for taunting Jesus. "Don't you fear God, even when you are dying?" Whether or not anything like this was actually said, the message is on-point. Both criminals were hours from death; "even when you are dying" meant "real soon."

---

[25] Single released by BNA Records on September 10, 2007; performed by artist Kenny Chesney; written by Casey Beathard and Chris Wallin.

[26] Directed by Franco Zeffirelli, written by Anthony Burgess, Suso Checchi d'Amico, and Franco Zeffirelli; starring Robert Powell; aired on Rai 1 (Italy) and NBC (United States), March 27–April 24, 1977.

Jesus, The Master Psychologist

Could those same words apply to us? We, too, are facing what Jesus' tormentor beside Him faced, if not real soon, someday. Whatever the time frame, "when" still fits.

Someone will ask me, "What puzzles you most about human behavior?" My answer, one might think, would lie somewhere along a lengthy litany of hearing people's struggles, tragedies, and inhumanities. While there is much I don't understand about human choices and motives, what I find hardest to understand is this: Why don't more people, particularly those nearing the end of this life, more earnestly ponder, "Who is God, and how do I get closer to Him?"

Later in life, some do ask, in the lyrics of a plaintive song, "What's it all about, Alfie? Is it just for the moment we live?"[27] Still, a baffling number don't appear to turn any closer to God than they did twenty, forty, or sixty years ago. Self-interest alone, that potent instinct wired so deeply within everyone, should compel them to do so. Why it doesn't is what puzzles me most. Not that I haven't pondered reasons.

My mother once answered my musings with, "I guess as long as you can still breathe easily, you think you're going to keep on breathing." A survey of the elderly confirms my mom's observation: No matter how old, if not in the midst of a life-threatening illness, most felt confident they would live at least another year. Therefore, death and what Christians believe instantly follows — judgment — is still some ways down the road. Put another way, there's no urgency quite yet.

Aging has been likened to a balloon always floating just ahead but never quite grasped. Upon reaching their elderly years, many don't see themselves as elderly. Others their age might be, but they're not. When old age is no longer old age, why think much about what might be coming after it?

---

[27] Burt Bacharach and Hal David, "Alfie."

Death? When?

"Sixty is the new forty." More are living robustly into and through years that not all that long ago were marked for slowing down. Medical advances and lifestyles have added an energy often belying chronological age. Activities once belonging to the younger are now pursued by the older.

Sixty may be the new forty, but I've found that nine o'clock is the new midnight. I still play softball, not in a senior league, but against players decades younger than me. Of course, there's been some decline, but I'm still able to compete. Sort of. When I had first started out, someone playing into his forties prompted us twenty-somethings to ask, "What's he doing out there on the field? He's going to get hurt." These days, the fields are filled with competent players in their forties and fifties. Stretched-out youth carries a sense of "Old age has receded. My last game is still seasons away."

Those who boldly declare there is no God (how would they know?), or who aren't sure whether or not to allow Him to exist, likewise don't spend time thinking about the hereafter. After all, if no God, then no Heaven, no Hell, just endless nothing. As one famous astronomer[28] preached, "The universe is all there is or ever was." How would he know?

Then, too, rather than God making us in His image, more people are making God in their image. Consequently, they assume that they are and will always be all right with God, for He sees them as they see themselves. He should welcome them into Heaven because, by their reckoning, they've earned it by being pretty good people, or at least not pretty bad people.

This attitude permeates funerals. The departed are almost always "with God," "in Heaven," "looking down on us," or "waiting for our reunion with them." While that might be true, it reflects a belief that Paradise awaits pretty much all of us, whether we love God

[28] Carl Sagan.

a lot or a little or not at all. While most definitely a comforting perspective, it may not align with God's.

Obviously, in the depths of grief, many would be quite reluctant to question someone's final destiny. Yes, we are to hope and pray for another's blessed end, knowing God is the judge. No, we are not to judge it settled. Nonetheless, as long as death is a guarantee of bliss, why the need to face it with a well-prepared soul?

A misguided fear of hypocrisy can push someone to keep God at arm's length to the very end. A friend of mine was an avowed agnostic. As she approached death, I approached her, "Who is Jesus to you?" She dodged the question, answering instead that she was not about to reverse a religion-free lifetime at the last minute. She saw it as a sign of integrity. Her attitude was, "This is how I lived; this is how I will die." How very sad that she totally misunderstood who Jesus is and how ready He is to open His arms to her at any time. Hers would not have been a renegotiation of her relationship with God. It would have been wise repentance.

Elisabeth Kübler-Ross, a psychiatrist, is known for studying how people react emotionally to imminent death. She predicted that most pass through a series of stages, those being denial, rage, bargaining, depression, and finally acceptance. In the first stage, one resists or denies his death. As death moves nearer, his emotions evolve until at last he accepts his inescapable fate.

To a Christian, "acceptance" is the hope of an incomprehensibly joyous new life. To a skeptic, it is a surrender to the unconquerable, the victor in the end.

Other researchers dispute Kübler-Ross's theory. They observe that most people don't follow her set stages. Some people interchange them. Some reverse them. Some skip rage or depression or bargaining with God for more life here.

In the end, the best predictor of how one dies is how one lived. If my life was a journey closer to God, then my journey's end will find me closer to Him. If I always elevated myself, neglecting Him, then death is my final adversary. The poet's words will haunt me, "Do not go gentle into that good night. Old age should burn and rave at close of day. Rage, rage against the dying of the light."[29]

My mother had a lifelong friend whom we'll call Annie. In her seventies, Annie was diagnosed with ovarian cancer. She never asked, "Why me?" Instead, she asked, "Why *not* me?" Annie was a woman of lifelong faith. Throughout her last weeks, she was confined to a hospital bed in her living room. During our last visit, she told me, "I've been given a good life. I'm grateful for all my blessings. I'm ready to head on." She was serene and at peace, with not a flicker of "rage against the dying of the light." My admiration for Annie, whose sons were my childhood friends, rose that much higher that day.

Imagine God tells you one morning that you will pass away in your sleep during the night. What's more, you are not to tell anyone about this. What would your last day look like? No doubt, you'd first decide to stay awake through the night. Beyond that, what would you do? Who would receive your time and how much? Who would hear of your love, your gratitude, your appreciation? What would you say that you should have said but didn't, and to whom? What regrettable words or actions would you seek to undo? Who would get the very best of you?

Of course, we can't live every day as if it were our last. Life's routines—raising children, working, eating, playing, planning, praying—make up much of our time. Yet thinking about how we would prioritize our last hours raises what an early television game show called its "$64,000 question," that is, its final question: If something is very good to do when our time to do it is short, why would it not be very good to do when our time is longer?

---

[29] Dylan Thomas, "Do Not Go Gentle into That Good Night."

Jesus, The Master Psychologist

Renewing and reconciling relationships may not seem quite so urgent when there's most likely another tomorrow. Lots of time remains to decide when and how to do what I should.

Let your priorities for your last day guide your priorities for all days. Life is not guaranteed, but death is. Live like you were dying so you can die like you lived.

About the Author

Dr. Ray Guarendi is a Catholic husband and father of ten adopted children, a clinical psychologist, author, professional speaker, and national radio and television host. His radio show, *The Dr. Is In*, can be heard on the EWTN Global Catholic Radio Network on over 350 stations and SiriusXM (channel 130). His TV show, *Living Right with Dr. Ray*, can be seen on EWTN television, reaching more than 350 million homes in 145 countries and territories.